Enrich others first, seek to get rich second. Or third.

TABLE OF CONTENTS

A New Day	vii
Is Hard Work Overrated?	1
The Goal of a Business Is to Make Money, but…	6
A Discussion about Life and Work	8
Help! I Don't Know My Passion!	37
My Issue with *The Secret*	40
Don't Call Yourself an Entrepreneur	42
Emotional Detachment Is a Good Thing	44
How Do the Rich Get Richer?	46
Pray for Riches?	49
Ageism and 40-Year-Olds	52
I Want You to Succeed. Do You?	54
Does It Take Money to Make Money?	56
The Best Way to Recover from Recessions	60
Why Do the Poor Get Poorer?	63
A Checklist for Starting Your Business	67
Final Words of Wisdom	70

A New Day

Why is hard work overrated? Like any platitude, it is vague and overused. No one is afraid of hard work, yet most people work jobs they dislike, and they are not where they want to be financially. That is why, in this book, I break down the deeper meaning of common platitudes in addition to lessons I learned from my mistakes as an entrepreneur.

This collection of thought-provoking essays is a composite of the knowledge I have gained over the years, most of it in the space of seven years or so. In that time, I spent $20,000 of my own money on a handful of failed businesses. In so doing, I have discovered many of the pain points and invisible chains that hold us in place not because they are so big. Rather, we either deny their existence or do not know they exist.

This book intentionally dives into specifics. It largely avoids generalities, such as abundance mindset, believe, hustle, get the word out there, work hard, grind, grit, determination, do whatever it takes, think big, attract it into your life, follow your passion, and many others.

If you are ready to grasp what is in this book, you will be enlightened, and more importantly, empowered to take the correct action with less fear and terror of the mistakes you will undoubtedly make along the way.

If you are not ready, most of it will seem like the same old stuff you have already heard, or it will make you angry or indignant, the way it did me when I first started awakening to much of it. Some lessons came from lectures given by self-made rich people and self-help experts; most came from the school of hard knocks and decades of watching people struggle, or flat out refuse, to accept these truths.

Growing up poor, I used to believe the myths that it took money to make money, all men are no good, God will bless you with money just because you are religious, rich people are the problem, if you have to work hard just to survive you must have to work *really hard* to get rich, so on and so forth.

The media outlets reinforce these myths, by the way.

To be honest, it took years of life beating me over the head with this wisdom to make me really and truly believe it and start thinking and moving in the right direction more consistently, as opposed to merely knowing the truth.

Or parroting the likes of Les Brown, Jim Rohn, and Tony Robbins.

I wrote this book because I believe there are people who can use my wisdom better than I have used it thus far. Just because I know it does not mean I am necessarily the best at utilizing it. The goal of a good teacher is to create new masters, not just apprentices who forever need to follow a master, never rising above the old master's level.

For the longest, I believed if I just had a good job and found the right woman, I would forget about the crazy, risky goal of starting a business, climbing that hill, and facing the stress and responsibilities. I was wrong. After about a decade, I had become frustrated with both corporate America and the whole dating scene.

This was the catalyst that initiated my eye-opening journey, the fruits of which are in this very book. Since my pursuit of money and a woman had morphed into my source of frustration, I did not have much to lose by risking these things to start a business.

I could have shut my eyes even longer if I had the distractions of a wife, children, and the pressing need to earn money to provide for them. I also could have shut them longer if I spent my twenties on sex, drugs, and alcohol.

Midlife crisis is not a point in a man's life when he wants to recapture his youth, divorce his wife and marry a blonde who is twenty years younger. Uh-uh.

Rather, midlife crisis is when a man (or anyone, for that matter) finally comes to grips with the fact he has been living a lie; trying to force himself to live someone else's life, living out someone else's ideals. It might take him until the age of twenty-five to reach this point; it might take him until the age of fifty-five. It all depends.

I spent so many years with my eyes shut tight and my hand in front of them to block out the light of truth, as it flew in the face of what I believed back then.

It is said people don't resist change; we resist *being changed.*

I urge you to believe everything in this book soon after you read it. Though you may not want to take it at face value without pondering it, I hope it does not take you over seven years to believe it when you can begin to benefit from it in less than one year.

Not to worry, you do not need to change your political affiliation, as politics are not the root cause of poverty and inequality, especially in the developed world, though many statistics are alarming. While rooted in facts, statistics are only a snapshot of what already is, not what is yet to be. Prior to 1920, it was a *fact* that women, even in America, were not allowed to vote save for women in the state of Utah.

When it comes to challenges and heartache, I have come to the realization that they are just as divinely ordained as glory. Suffering, on its own, does not lead to glory; you must create ways in your mind to draw from wisdom gained during the suffering to know what to do when you face these same challenges on the bumpy road to glory.

While the objective of this book is completely about putting you in the driver's seat, God's role is definitely worth discussing.

When we pray for, or want something, it is as though God tells us the steps we need to take, usually through inclination and whispers of intuition. You will not always hear Him correctly, but He gave us free will and less-than-crystal-clear foresight for a reason. However, I truly believe it is easier to hear God when we stop praying for things, circumstances, and people to show up (or go away, for that matter). We have two ears and one mouth for a reason.

He gives us the correct steps when we need to know them, not the ones we want to take or when we want to know the steps. It is imperative we continue to take steps and make mistakes in order to continue receiving the necessary steps from God. When we stop moving, He stops talking.

Once you reach the end of this guide, you will know whether you personally should seek enjoyment and fulfillment from a job, and perhaps a side hustle, or double down as an entrepreneur and venture into the unknown. More importantly, you will know you made the right choice, the good choice, regardless of which path you desire.

Is Hard Work Overrated?

I will tell you how you should work instead.

Using real estate as an example, most of us work hard at things like learning the market, giving better walkthroughs, and asking the broker for leads.

So, we do these things for a few months, get frustrated with our lack of progress, then we double down with the learning and asking for leads. Finally, after continued hard work (and lack of progress), we start to assume you need to know somebody, or you need to do some unseemly things to become successful. When we go through this losing cycle, it feels as though we have tried *everything,* and *nothing* seems to work.

A person in this situation is treating the broker like an employer. There is a difference. An employer is, in a sense, "obligated" to provide you with enough work to feed your family. A broker is not.

An employer creates the work. As an employee, you only need to show up, do the work, and get paid. As an entrepreneur or real-estate agent, *you must create the work*, then show up, do the work, and *possibly* get paid.

The answers to the foregoing include the likes of cold calling prospects and getting connected with the right people.

This *is* the "hard work" required to be successful in business and real estate; it is where the rubber meets the road.

But most of us are so terrified of doing these things, we secretly hope if we just work really, really hard at hounding the broker for leads, and learning how to give great walkthroughs we can mostly or entirely avoid the cold calling and getting connected with strangers. We hope the broker will send us that *one lead* whom we can amaze by working hard at crisscrossing town and giving great walkthroughs—a lead who will kickstart our reputation and flow of commissions without cold calling or getting connected with strangers. Consequently, most of us do not get what we want, no matter how badly we want it, no matter how badly we hate our current circumstances, and no matter how hard we work.

This is true even for most social butterflies who never meet a stranger. Making friends is great, but making connections is terrifying; it is a much bigger responsibility. You only need to chat and drink booze to make friends and forge an emotional connection to keep them. However, you need to turn cold calls into hot leads and use them to help other professionals complete *their* deals if you want to make connections. This is certainly how real estate works.

There is an entire "cold calling is dead" industry funded by our fear and terror of placing cold calls and getting connected with strangers. This industry sells expensive monthly services such as ringless voicemail (robocalls), so you can avoid being cursed out or hung up on.

Which vital activities, in your industry, if any, are you running away from? Are you working too hard on some activities, trying in vain to compensate for the ones you just do not want to perform? Ask yourself these questions every day you do not achieve the level of success you desire at school, work, et cetera.

So, how can you push yourself to perform the likes of these activities? For starters, just relax. Don't worry about getting it wrong. Make it okay, in your mind, to get it wrong and be extremely uncomfortable until you do it enough times to get it right. Mistakes become mere memories given enough time. Do not worry about how much time it will take to get it right, just work to get incrementally better.

Now, I will let you in on a little secret: for most of us, reasons such as hating our jobs, wanting more money, and wanting lifestyle freedom are <u>not</u> strong enough to get us to wholeheartedly perform such activities.

Ironically, these weak reasons are the same ones many network marketing companies and life coaches use to pull people in. They use other weak reasons, such as providing for your family or having extra income. For most of us, these reasons are just strong enough to push us out of bed so we can go to some job, maybe two jobs, and earn a paycheck.

Such reasons are not strong enough to push most of us to be successful entrepreneurs, and that's okay. Just keep reading.

Do you have any reasons bigger than <u>your</u>self and <u>your</u> family? For example, Bill Gates and Paul Allen back in the '70s decided they wanted to put a personal computer on every desk, on a planet with about four billion people at the time. This is not a great philanthropic mission. However, bringing such a useful, yet unproven, product to the world was so important to <u>them</u>, they sacrificed the college degrees they themselves could have earned.

It took Gates, Allen, and their team twelve years to build Microsoft into a large company and take it public.

If you do not have any big reasons like this, it's okay. Embracing the major challenges and appreciating who you are becoming as a result of the struggle are vital to your success without some sort of passion to pull you through. If you do not embrace the challenge, you will become one of those *miserable rich people* whom we love to talk about, especially when we are short on cash.

Or you will just give up.

Now, let us break down the likes of cold calling and getting connected with the right people. As for cold calling, you need to understand who could use your services, and why. As for getting connected with the right people, one must review the different capacities within his or her chosen industry.

Once again, using good ol' real estate as an example, potential prospects include empty nesters, landlords, rehabbers, properties for sale by owner (FSBOs), people facing foreclosure, as well as owners of deleted listings, and listings over ninety days old.

The right people in real estate to get connected with include other agents, landlords and rehabbers, as well as linchpin people needed to close a transaction, such as a loan officer and a real-estate attorney.

Who are the right people to get connected with in your industry? Make a list of five to ten types of people.

So, going back to potential prospects, there are websites that, for a fee, will allow you to filter properties by the potential equity, as well as physical features and locations. These sites also reveal the names and phone numbers of the homeowners. You can also find when the house was purchased.

An empty nester will likely have a lot of equity and have lived in the home for over twenty years, as an example.

To find the other prospects mentioned, you don't really need to pay for subscription services. Landlords have their numbers in house-rental ads. Well-to-do landlords and rehabbers attend property auctions and must pay in cash to acquire properties. County websites give the names and mailing addresses of property owners for free. Ownership information about a house bought at auction will be updated when the title is transferred to the highest bidder.

FSBOs are on websites such as Craigslist and BuyOwner. However, if you go this route, I suggest having a cash buyer already lined up and willing to pay close to asking price, since people go the FSBO route to save thousands in commissions and get more money in their pockets. A cash buyer who isn't trying to drive a hard bargain could potentially make the owner of a FSBO more amenable to using your services.

Homes in foreclosure will be listed on county websites. However, be sure to research liens and back taxes to make sure the property is not upside down. Research videos on topics such as "Fiverr title search" to help you secure cheap preliminary title searches to determine if a property is worth your time.

Listings over ninety days old, as well as removed listings can be found on the MLS website or Zillow.com. When going this route, listening to the seller and effectively articulating how you will help this person are paramount, since this homeowner has "been here before," with the subject property.

In your industry, what are some questions you should ask every prospect? Do you have a series of open-ended questions to quickly gauge a customer's general needs and desires, as well as a series of yes/no questions to help you provide the best product or service for that person's wants or needs? Assuming you only had one minute with each new prospect, what two or three questions would you ask?

I suggest creating a form with these questions, along with fields for the person's name and address, the features of the property being sold, the features of the property the prospect wants to buy, as well as a notes section for the prospect's unique circumstances, and reasons for selling and/or buying.

The notes section, regardless of your industry, will contain the powerful, emotional reasons driving your prospect's wants and needs. Use this section for unique items and concerns that do not really have a place in a standard form. The quality of the notes taken will vary between someone who listens to the customer versus someone who merely hears the customer.

Keep plenty of blank copies of this form at home, work, and in the car so you will be ready whenever someone calls you, or you call them. You can even take cellphone pictures of completed forms or keep completed hard copies in a brightly-colored hollow clipboard if you want to have them close by for quick editing and indexing. This way, your prospects will not have to repeat themselves every time they call you.

Now, for getting connected with the right people. Sites such as Meetup.com feature groups of people in various industries who periodically meet in person. Real-estate professionals may belong to a real-estate investors' association (REIA).

Some networking experts have suggested we pick a small group of people, make them our first contacts when we have a deal and invite them to coffee or lunch once or twice a month, as opposed to mindlessly handing out business cards to a bunch of people and hoping some of them will give us a call.

Furthermore, I would suggest working with your connections in a spirit of, "How can I help <u>you</u> get richer?" This is especially powerful for a newcomer to an industry. Successful people often have wannabes tugging at their coattails or hanging around hoping some of the successful person's success rubs off on them somehow. If that were the case, live-in maids and cooks would not die poor.

Many of us believe that the rich getting richer is a bad thing. Therefore, a person who wants to help a wealthy connection become wealthier, as opposed to only leveraging their wealthy connections and giving little in return, will be a welcome breath of fresh air.

So, basically, working the right way involves learning the work and technical skills involved with your industry (things we are comfortable doing), learning about the needs of the customer/client and those of the players in the industry (things that make us uncomfortable), and wholeheartedly *reaching out* to them and serving them, as opposed to playing the game of *build it and they will come*.

The Goal of a Business Is to Make Money, But...

Some people work to create goods and services customers will spend money on. Meanwhile, others work to create goods and services customers want so badly, they will do anything to have those goods and services, including spending their hard-earned cash.

While both objectives involve getting the customer to buy something, they are not the same. Though slightly different from each other, the second objective will yield much better results for the same entrepreneur, attempting to sell the same types of products and services.

The first objective will cause someone to imitate something another company is "making money from," and shove the imitation down customers' throats. However, the second objective would cause someone to ask questions, such as:

1. "Is my product fun, useful, or necessary?"
2. "Is this really the best I can make it, or am I just trying to make a buck as soon as possible, so I can quit my day job as soon as possible?"

Moreover, the second objective will inspire the entrepreneur to conduct better product surveys and host well-organized focus group meetings, as opposed to shoving an inferior product down the customers' throats in a feeble attempt to just make money as soon as possible without having to deal with people that much.

Focus group attendees who are not remunerated are more likely to express their true sentiments about your product or service than those who are paid for their opinions. Unpaid attendees do not have a subconscious debt of gratitude driving them to exaggerate the virtues of your product, minimize its shortcomings, or downplay its competitors.

A Discussion About Life and Work

Have you thought of your financial goals in detail? For example, have you pondered whether you want to be wealthy and powerful (worth $100 million or more), rich and comfortable (worth seven or eight figures), or if you simply want to be comfortable and pay your bills (nice home in the suburbs, able to send your kids to college)?

Do you want to be rich or well off? Do you not really care to be rich but just want to be your own man or woman and not have to work for someone else?

These questions, and the true, brutally honest answers to them are critical, as the path to each one is a bit different.

If you want to be wealthy and powerful, your company most likely needs to have a global reach. If you want to be wealthy or well off, you must become an effective leader, motivator, disciplinarian, team builder, team player, and a good judge of one's character and abilities.

This is important, because you will need a lot of employees to serve a lot of customers and earn a lot of money and credibility if you want to be rich. The employees you keep on the payroll and the behavior and performance you accept from them is how you represent <u>yourself</u> and your company to customers.

If you just want to work for yourself and do not care to be rich, you just have to be a good leader of yourself. And you don't need a global or even a state-wide reach.

A Discussion About Life and Work

There is no such thing as "get rich quick." You know the cliché about the lottery winner who wins a bunch of money and is broke in five to ten years, or the athlete who wastes his money in the same way.

Did you know many of these people lose a lot of money in their ill-guided attempts to use their <u>money to make money</u>, as opposed to spending on cars, houses, paying off relatives' debts, and buying crap?

This is because they are trying too hard to *avoid being the cliché spendthrift*. In addition, they depend too much upon money to make them richer, while gathering too little education and wisdom before investing gradually larger sums of money into a certain type of investment.

They think, "It takes money to make money, so, I will use my <u>money</u> to buy a fixer-upper, <u>pay</u> architects to devise a new layout, <u>pay</u> contractors to do the dirty work, and <u>pay</u> an interior designer to stage the home, so I can sell it and make <u>more money</u> in this rapidly gentrifying neighborhood."

Or, they may think, "I have $20 million. I can buy this 200-unit apartment complex for $15 million and rent out each unit for an average of $1,100 per month, make over $200k per month, and recover my investment in about seven years depending on occupancy rates. And I'll still have a $5-million cushion."

They jump right in, as opposed to starting off by learning from experts who have successfully done what they want to do, then starting off with smaller investments so that any beginner's mistakes will also be smaller, but just as educational as making the same mistakes with a larger amount of money.

And some people do take it slow for about two or three deals, then push all their chips on the table for some megadeal. Why? Because many of us have the poisonous mindset of, "I want so much money, I <u>never have to work</u> again." When we think and work in this way, we are hyper focused on taking shortcuts we believe will allow us to sit back and collect checks in the mail ASAP, as opposed to thinking and working toward being a preeminent expert in the field.

A preeminent expert who is committed to working and becoming the best, even long after most people would want to retire from work, will earn as much money as he or she wants.

For example, Warren Buffett (worth over $100 billion) is in his nineties, and still manages his company, Berkshire Hathaway. Dr. Dre had enough money to retire in the early 1990s, but he is still active. Betty White acted for seventy-five years before she retired. If their major goal were to have "so much money they never had to work again," they would not have accomplished what they have.

Why? First, you neither do your absolute best work, nor make the best decisions when your eyes are on the door, looking for an exit. Your eyes need to be on the task at hand, and your chosen industry as a whole.

Second, the road to riches is not paved with money, and the difficulties encountered on that road will stop anyone who focuses too much on money itself, and too little on the business or career path. The more you focus on money itself, the more money you will waste trying to build your business or career as quickly as possible, so you *never have to work again* as quickly as possible.

Third, you set shallow roots in your chosen industry because you are looking for a quick getaway no more than five to ten years down the road. As in, you don't bother to get connected with customers or forge alliances with industry insiders. This is along the lines of hounding the broker for leads and learning how to give great walkthroughs, as opposed to connecting with potential clients and forging alliances with other real-estate professionals.

Although Kylie Jenner became a billionaire at age twenty-one, after four years of building her cosmetics line, the whole process was not that short.

It actually started many years prior when Kris Jenner's first husband, Robert Kardashian Sr., along with Johnnie Cochran, defended Orenthal "OJ" Simpson in the sensational 1994 trial for his alleged murder of Nicole Brown Simpson.

"If the glove doesn't fit, you must acquit." – Johnnie Cochran (1937-2005).

Then, about a decade later, one of Kylie's older sisters was seen in a leaked sex tape. Finally, the Kardashian/Jenner family got a reality TV show in 2007, predating Kylie's cosmetics line by seven years. Nothing against Kylie; just don't get mad when your business does not make you rich after a few years.

Chinese construction workers can erect skyscrapers in six to twenty days, as opposed to the usual two to five years it takes in America. That's only partly true. The Chinese buildings are assembled from prefabricated parts.

Steve Jobs was the CEO of a billion-dollar company when he was only twenty-five, in 1980. That is true, but he, Steve Wozniak, and many others worked tirelessly to grow Apple for six years beforehand. Most tech companies do not achieve success that quickly, not even Microsoft.

Another thing: life beats most people over the head with lessons before they become wealthy. Life allowed Jobs to become wealthy first, then get beat over the head with life lessons, much like it does with a wildly-successful seventeen-year-old drug dealer. After years of battles with other managers, Jobs was kicked out of Apple in 1985. This marked the beginning of his transformative twelve-year hiatus before his return to the company.

Moreover, in 1968 at age twelve (in Steve's own words), he phoned Bill Hewlett of Hewlett-Packard. He wanted spare parts to build a frequency counter. That summer, he had an internship with the company. Tech managed to become an obsession for him—a part of who he is.

Many people with tech startups are just trying to become "the next Bill Gates or Steve Jobs," by writing a little code, and using a lot of venture capital to pay programmers for whom writing code is solely a way to make money. The programmers have accomplished their goal regardless of how your tech startup fares. However, Bill Gates, Steve Jobs, and Mark Zuckerberg did the opposite to get where they are.

Are you obsessed with your desired level of success, and more importantly, <u>your chosen field of endeavor</u>? Many of us are obsessed with being financially successful, being our own boss, or being an entrepreneur, but we do not have any real chosen field. We are willing to do "whatever it takes, or anything, or anything within reason" to become successful.

It is fine to want massive success. However, your desire to excel and be the best in your chosen field should be *even stronger* than your desire for massive success. This is because everyone wants massive success. Therefore, if wealth and success are more important to you than the industry, you are on a level playing field with people who remain poor or average, not those who achieve massive success.

Rap artists who are both gifted and tenacious, who just want money and a better life are the rare exception to this rule because they are so few and far between, the supply/demand ratio ensures they earn large incomes in spite of their mindset. They may not become P. Diddy or Jay Z, but they will become well off nonetheless.

This is contrary to people trying their hand at real estate, designing T-shirts, or being their own boss so they don't have to work for somebody. These types of people are a dime a dozen, and therefore, a textbook example of the rule. This group also includes rappers who are gifted but not so tenacious, or vice versa, as compared to rap artists who become megastars.

I know because I tried all these things myself primarily in a feeble attempt to "make money," the way some of you have. (Yes, I even plunked out a handful of rap beats with FL Studio.)

Think about it. There are literally a gazillion different ways and industries out there you can be a part of and "make money." That is why your immediate goal should be to narrow your options as hard as you can to one option, or a very closely-related family of options. Do not keep your options open.

If you keep your options open, you have given yourself the option to run away when one field of endeavor becomes too difficult – or – stirs up fears or negative emotions when you are at the cusp of success. If your options are severely limited, however, you are forced to draw up the courage to push through the fears (perhaps some tears, too) and negative emotions, and reach the success on the other side.

If you are "willing to do anything," or feel as if, "I will do it if I can make money, or if people will pay me for it," that can be likened to the character in a slasher flick running aimlessly in the woods trying to go "anywhere but the cabin with the chainsaw-wielding psychopath in it."

The character gets lost, looks around, then meets their terrible fate. Our chances for success usually meet the same fate when we are *willing to do anything*.

Now, re-imagine the prior scene: The character came to the cabin from the main road, and using a compass, noted that his bearing was 110 degrees ESE. Next, the killer starts chasing him, but this time, the character <u>knows where he is and where he wants to go</u>. We must do this in our own lives in order to achieve the level of success we want.

Since the character knows his original bearing from the road was 110 degrees ESE, he knows he needs to run in the opposite direction 180 degrees away, or 290 degrees WNW to get back to the road.

The character makes it to the road and runs across it. The chainsaw-wielding killer tries to do the same, but he gets hit by an 80,000-pound fully-loaded tractor-trailer (piloted by someone normal, by the way) traveling at sixty miles per hour! The character lives.

While it is good to know how to do many things and know how to work seamlessly with many different types of people, there comes a time when you must pick a direction and specialize in that direction if you want high levels of success. You can later venture out into another field of endeavor once you have become a five- or ten-year veteran of the first field of endeavor. And hire the right help. This is how a person can successfully own and operate multiple unrelated businesses.

Hard work is the path to success. Well, that depends. What do you consider hard work? More importantly, **what do you consider success**?

We have heard our whole lives that hard work is the path to success. The hard work to keep a marriage strong. The hard work to get rich. The hard work to get big and buff. The hard work to provide for a family. The hard work to earn a college degree.

Let's face it, most people say they "worked hard" to get where they are because they don't want to appear lazy, entitled, or as if success was *just handed to them,* somehow. We don't want to appear soft.

Instead of trying to "work hard," we must ***wholeheartedly perform the necessary work***, based on what we want to accomplish. Have you seen the scene from *The Pursuit of Happyness* (2006) when Chris Gardner saw a man driving a new Ferrari, and asked him, "What do you do and how do you do it?"

Asking this question is the fastest way to learn just what the necessary work is, and how to do it. Push a knowledgeable person to speak in specifics, not generalities, such as hard work, sacrifice, and giving it all you got.

Not only did Chris Gardner do everything the man told him, he did so *wholeheartedly*, in spite of the very real risk of failure with brokering stocks, on top of his failure with selling portable bone density scanners, and his failed relationship with his son's mother.

Wholeheartedly means Mr. Gardner did not attempt to get into real estate, and moonlight as a bartender, while working as a stockbroker, in an attempt to have something to fall back on, the way most of us would.

Consider which one of the statements below would make you, or most people more likely to admire a rich person:

1. "I was born into a poor family, and I worked hard, and I fought and clawed for many years to amass my fortune. I wasn't born with a silver spoon in my mouth."
2. "When I was twenty-nine years old, I pushed through my fear of writing business plans and my fear of rejection. Then, I went to 400 investment bankers in my city and eventually pieced together enough financing to buy land and materials and hire some hard-working guys to build my first apartment complex. I spent many years 'rinsing and repeating,' so to speak, to amass my fortune."

The first statement would resonate with most people, since most of us look down on someone who just went out and secured funding or went out and decided to *get to know* the right people, even if this person was born into a poor family.

When we are poor, we tend to believe and say things about rich people such as, "She probably pleasured some old rich creep. All those rich people knew somebody. All those rich people have a crooked daddy or granddaddy who started the family fortune." And on, and on, and on.

Now, back to hard work. If you want to be wealthy in, say, construction, you could work hard, learn the trade, then <u>teach and lead your own group of employees</u> after years of hard work.

Or you could take the Andrew Carnegie route: make it a point to get acquainted with wealthy, powerful people, then spend ten years in administrative positions within their companies, helping *them* get *even richer*.

Carnegie started doing this when he was a twelve-year-old telegraph boy, delivering telegrams to powerful men. Other hungry immigrant boys in Pittsburgh delivered telegrams to the same wealthy, powerful men as well. However, they were so focused on the sprint to alleviate their hunger, they never really thought about the marathon to own the farm.

This is where most of us get in trouble. Since we are wired for survival of self and survival of species, earning $0.25 to $0.50 a day to deliver telegrams definitely solves the immediate need for food and shelter, in spite of the fact it is not the road to riches. Very few people become rich, due to the simple fact that being wealthy is not a prerequisite for survival, and therefore, is not typically treated as a pressing need.

While the other boys may have delivered more telegrams and earned more money in the here and now, Carnegie made himself more valuable to Pittsburgh's industrialists by learning key aspects of their businesses. He could also listen to Morse code and transcribe messages as they came over the telegraph line, as opposed to sifting through ribbons of printed messages and using a chart to transcribe them afterwards.

In the long run, Carnegie's method was very beneficial to him. By the time he was about sixty-five years old, his net worth mushroomed to over $300 million (nominal terms, 1901), during a time when the average steelworker was only paid about $700 a year.

If only maids, nannies, and other telegraph boys bothered to *become acquainted* with their rich clients like Carnegie did.

A rich person will be more likely to give you financial backing for your good ideas if you have helped them get richer, especially if you gather people with the correct knowledge and experience to properly execute your good ideas.

Countless people vomit at the idea of working to help the rich get richer, even though many of us want to get rich ourselves! Many of us forget all about the old platitude, "Treat others the way you want to be treated," when it comes to this.

Andrew Carnegie is the second-richest American in history (net worth as a share of the US economy at the time) due to owning steel mills, but the 5'3" Scottish immigrant never worked in one of those hot, noisy deathtraps for twelve hours a day, six days a week like his employees. He did not create any revolutionary steelmaking processes, either.

Carnegie profited from an innovation by Englishman Henry Bessemer. The steel town of Bessemer, Alabama near Birmingham was named after Henry.

Andrew Carnegie simply believed steel should replace cast iron in bridges, railroads, and tall buildings because of steel's higher tensile strength (resistance to breaking) as compared to cast iron.

Most of us work hard at the wrong things throughout our careers. If you perform entry-level work for forty years, sure, you may have helped your employer earn millions, but since you did not lead any employees or make any big decisions, the company did not pay you very much.

Why? Well, most of us are terrified of leadership roles and their responsibilities, while very few of us are willing to be the captain of the ship and be responsible for other adult human beings. It's all about supply and demand.

Most of us can be likened to the person who says he or she wants to make it in Hollywood, but they are driving 160 miles per hour on Interstate 10…east, trying to get there from Houston, Texas! No matter how hard you drive, or how many years you drive, you will never get to Hollywood from Texas by driving on I-10 due east.

Meanwhile, the person who is driving some thirty-year-old rust bucket at sixty-five miles per hour on Interstate 10 *west* will make it to California a lot faster. Why? Because they are traveling in the right direction (working on the right activities conducive to reaching their stated goals).

The eastbound driver is someone who works an entry-level job, sometimes two at a time, for forty years trying to become well off, without even learning how to invest their money and make it work for them, instead of the other way around.

We would be better off cutting down our expenses so we may spend less time and energy earning a paycheck, and spend more time improving ourselves to the point where we can properly lead and serve enough people to become wealthy without *"killing ourselves"* spending 100 hours a week on the job.

It takes money to make money. Wrong. The more of yourself you spend to promote your business and improve your products and services, the less money you need. If you are good with meeting new people not just as friends but also selling them on your ability to help them, that is a plus.

Also, learn as much as you can about your customer and about human nature in general. For starters, everyone wants to be heard, <u>understood</u>, and to receive some level of empathy. We also want to feel needed and <u>important</u>.

The customer is always boss. When you work for a company, you just have intermediate bosses between yourself and the ultimate boss (customer). If you cannot give the ultimate boss what he or she wants, they will fire you or your company by taking their business elsewhere. Some small business owners, such as those who air dirty laundry in the presence of customers or who are late for appointments with clients either do not know this truth or ignore it, and in return, secure their own mediocrity at best.

An angry dissatisfied customer who gives you a piece of their mind is better for your business than a "nice" dissatisfied customer, if you can handle negative criticism and use it to improve your ways of conducting business.

"Nice" dissatisfied customers will just go somewhere else, never to return to you again, without giving you any feedback about what is killing your referral opportunities and repeat business. Referrals and repeat business are the biggest sources of revenue for companies and salespeople. These sources also dramatically cut down on the need to advertise.

I work so hard to provide for myself and my family. Why do I struggle, while the rich keep getting richer? I have come to the painful realization that most of us never reach our full potential <u>because</u> we work to provide for *our*selves and *our* families, and don't give a (four-letter word) about the customers, the employer, or our co-workers, just as long as we get our paycheck. This attitude keeps us poor because providing for ourselves and our families does not add value for the customer/client or an employer.

So many of us are so busy trying to avoid kissing someone's rear end, we do not go the extra mile for employers (or new, unproven, or small-time customers if we have our own business). Many large corporations take on this attitude as well. This ensures our mediocrity in our chosen field of endeavor, since that is how most everyone else thinks and, in turn, behaves.

Both of these attitudes ensure our mediocrity because, let's face it, most people work to provide for *them*selves and *their* families, or start a business to follow *their* passion so *they* don't have to work some job *they* hate. If you do not rise above the attitude (deep-seated thoughts, feelings, and actions) of most people, you will have the same results as most people.

We work hard to make money. We go to college, take on a second job, or start a business to make *more* money. We say money is the root of all evil but, in the same breath, wish for a lottery win or a bigger paycheck. We pray to God for a lottery win or just an end to our money woes in general. Therefore, the rich are not the main ones who only care about money. Sure, the poor don't poison the environment or exploit illegal workers, but the foregoing is still true.

When most of us get into stocks or real estate, we are more excited about the money we can earn than we are about becoming the best at stocks or real estate. Rich people are the opposite. That is why they are rich.

While Microsoft co-founders Bill Gates and the late Paul Allen undoubtedly enjoyed their billions of dollars, their main reason for starting Microsoft was to put "a computer [no doubt pre-loaded with Microsoft programs] on every desk and in every home." That is a tall challenge to rise to on a planet that had over four billion people in 1975. But they rose to it anyway. That is why they are billionaires. They did not think, "Oh, I don't want to kill myself," like most of us would. If you feel you are about to die, you can drink more water and eat more vegetables. You can be ambitious and take care of your body at the same time.

Furthermore, a fear of "killing yourself" is an undeniable sign that your current reasons for accomplishing what you set out to accomplish are not very deep or compelling to you personally, though they may be for someone else.

Also, being organized will allow you to make the most of your time and energy. For example, have an agenda and questions written down before placing any phone calls or hosting any staff meetings. Plan your days and weeks in advance. Why spend eighteen hours a day working if you can accomplish the same **objectives** by working twelve or fourteen hours a day? Or less?

Most of us want to start a business so "I have so much money I never have to work another day in my life, or so I can be my own boss." These mindsets scream for failure because, let's face it, they take your focus off the people who are vital to making you rich in the first place: your customers, employees, and business partners.

Furthermore, these mindsets cause us to put in as little creativity as possible and grow and change as a person as little as possible, while expecting the best outcome possible. It does not matter how hard you work if you are just making crap with little creativity, and with little to average regard for the person on the receiving end.

I found that out the hard way when I started a toy company primarily to make so much money, I never had to work again. I merely created a poor imitation of what successful companies such as Fisher-Price sold. Why? I figured, "They made money from selling toys. Why can't I?"

Moreover, Mattel sold enough Barbies to have $4 billion to buy Kevin O'Leary's *The Learning Company* in May 1999.

Worse yet, I spent too much money on supplies and technology in wishful anticipation of the company taking off like a rocket, and, in turn, giving me so much money, I never had to work again quite soon. Some of you are in this boat.

Is your business just churning out poor imitations of what another company is successfully selling? Are you just trying to be the "next Twitter or Amazon"?

Fear is the Master of Disguise. You read that right. Many of us use all sorts of reasons to avoid reaching our goals or rising into our greatness:

A death in the family. Our kid is acting up. Nobody is buying my products or services. I'm tired. I don't have enough money. The economy is bad. I can't focus on that right now. I need to find a girlfriend, and too many others to list in one lifetime.

Why do we cook up any reasons at all? We have a few basic fears, including:

1. Fear of failure or looking bad. (Failure)
2. Fear of someone harming us or those we care about. (Success)
3. Fear of family and friends suddenly having money problems only you can solve. (Success)

4. Fear of attracting groupies and gold diggers. (Success)
5. Fear of those close to us becoming jealous. (Success)
6. Fear of our friends thinking...we think...we are too good for them. (Success)
7. Fear of extra stress, pressure, and responsibility. (Success)
8. Fear of being cussed out by superiors or big clients while climbing the corporate ladder. (Success)
9. Fear of being in the public eye, lack of privacy. (Success)
10. Fear of becoming successful, just to lose it all and end up back where you started, which is worse than having never been successful in the first place! (Success and Failure)
11. Fear of missing out, fear of better options. (Less success than we could've had)
12. Fear of becoming rich and miserable! (Success)
13. Fear of abusing our power like a pedophile in power! (Success)
14. Fear of becoming some monster we despise! (Success)

If you noticed, most of our fears are not the fear of failure but the fear of success. How can we overcome these fears? Realize these things happen to *way, way* more everyday citizens than rich people.

Being poor or middle class is just as risky as being rich! Most people who are murdered are poor or middle class. Most people who are raped or kidnapped are not rich. Most of the awful criminals who do these things are not rich.

Money is just a magnifier of who and what you are, good, bad, or indifferent. Many people who are rich or upper-middle class and miserable started off poor and unhappy (or miserable). It ain't the money's fault.

Some of us unconsciously create businesses that need an unrealistic amount of volume in order to be profitable. It sounds crazy at first glance. However, it prevents us from ever having to face our fears, and we still get to feel as if we are working hard toward something worthwhile. "I'm not like 'the masses' glued to social media and television; I'm an *entrepreneur*. I'm on my *grind*," we get to tell ourselves. You can easily spin your wheels for decades doing this.

It takes a lot of energy to be tired. "I'm tired. God, I'm sleepy!" This is what you will hear your co-workers, maybe even yourself say during a typical workday. There is a word for it all: *Lies!*

When we are disengaged from or disinterested in our current activity, our minds shut down.

This is because disengagement, disinterest, and other negative emotions such as thinking about how *tired* you are, reduce the dopamine levels in our brains. Dopamine is not just a feel-good chemical; it also controls skeletal muscle function and energy levels.

Caffeine keeps you awake, not because it increases dopamine levels. No, no. It stimulates your adrenal glands. Adrenaline is normally secreted when we need to fight or flee. Basically, drinking coffee to stay awake during the workday makes our brains function as if we are trying to outrun a serial killer or a hungry lion for eight hours. That'll keep you awake!

Now, do you understand why there is so much malaise and discontent in America, even though our poorest citizens eat something every day and are rich or well off as compared to two-thirds of the world's people? #FirstWorldProblems.

What is the solution to all of this? Follow your passion? Not necessarily. The solution is to become passionate about being the best at your current activity, even if it is not "your passion." Something else: Stop thinking about how tired you are. Just stand up straight and focus on the task at hand.

Thinking about how tired you are only makes you *more tired!* Tired is just a state of mind, 80 or 90% of the time. Think about it. Most people are *so tired* and even yawning when they are at work, but then, they magically perk up when they leave work and go home! They were never tired; their dopamine levels were a tad depressed.

Being committed to accomplishing big, major goals, bigger than yourself and your family will also give you a lot more energy.

Tired (yawn) is just a state of mind.

Money is a means, not an end. The great thinker, Earl Nightingale (1921-1989) said it best when he said, "We confuse means with ends."

Robert Plant, in Led Zeppelin's song, *Ten Years Gone* (1975), said, "...though the course may change sometimes, rivers always reach the sea..."

Basically, the <u>means</u> to an end may have to change sometimes, but the ends should remain the same. For instance, if you do not have lots of money sitting around to start your business, you can set up your business so the customer buys the parts up front, then pays you for labor. That way, you have very small cash outlays up front.

Did you know this is how enterprise computer assembly companies work? The customer, usually a gigantic tech company, buys the computer components and instructs the manufacturer to ship them to the computer assembly company. Once assembled, the computer assembly company ships them to the customer's data centers.

This is why the customers send nasty emails to the assembly company's supervisors when employees accidentally throw $1,500 motherboards in the trash or break components. (Remember, the customer is the boss, and can fire the computer assembly company at will.)

They pay the assembly company for labor, overhead, and the convenience of not having to deal with the HR challenge of high employee turnover inherent in warehouses; storage of parts and incomplete computer assemblies (less space efficient than completed computer assemblies); or the liability risk of <u>directly</u> employing data center staff *and* computer assembly staff. Fewer employees on their own premises and payroll translates into a lower liability risk.

This convenience, or value-add, gives the computer assembly company the "right" to charge enough money to turn a handsome profit, not just break even with expenses. This is true for any individual or company that adds enough value for the customer or client.

Gold is real, but its value is just as imaginary as that of fiat currency not backed by gold. Or the value of anything else, for that matter.

The value of anything is imaginary, and relative to the value we assign, in our minds, to other things. This includes relationships, money, material things, and immaterial things. For instance, your house is worth $200,000; a sack of potatoes is worth $2.50; and your car cost $25,000. So, you see, <u>in our minds</u>, a car is worth 10,000 times as much as a sack of potatoes, a house is worth 200,000 times a dollar, and a sack of potatoes is worth two and one-half times a dollar.

And a dollar is worth over 100 Japanese yen. They are both backed by nothing, or faith and confidence to put it lightly, so why is one yen worth a lot less than a dollar? Japan also has a robust, diverse economy. In fact, Japan boasted the world's second-largest economy from 1968 to 2010.

Well, that difference in value is because billions of people the whole world over have been persuaded to believe so, by a handful of people in government, central banks, and the foreign exchange market.

Since value is imaginary, a celebrity or athlete can earn more money than a doctor or a schoolteacher. Why? This is because we value entertainers (or being entertained) more than our health and education. Well, we notice our moods every day, but we notice and acknowledge the limitations of our health and education a lot less often. Moreover, there are fewer NBA players than there are doctors and teachers.

Imagine people, the likes of Kobe Bryant, teaching classes of 10,000 kids. They would want more than $55,000 a year. There are about 10,000 K-12 students per every professional athlete in America.

You can't always get what you want, but if you try sometimes, you just might find...you get what you really and truly believe you are <u>worthy</u> and <u>capable</u> of, deep in your heart, regardless of what your mouth may say.

We are all a product of the <u>least</u> we will accept for ourselves, regardless of the lofty goals we may have.

If you want better, you have to say to yourself, with conviction, "I am going to do this, whether <u>I</u> like it or not!"

Don't worry about "them" or "they," for you are completely responsible for the actions you take or do not take. All "they" can do is talk, whether they are positive people or negative people.

Although Tyler Perry was homeless for a few years after he moved to Atlanta, he worked on himself to the point that making hit movies and owning a studio is the least he would accept for himself.

The least you will accept is like a thermostat. Tyler Perry was homeless, but his thermostat was set to "wealthy mogul." That is why he eventually became wealthy. The journey was hard on him emotionally, but he eventually made it.

The thermostats of many homeless people are set to "as long as I'm breathing." A welfare recipient's thermostat is set to "at least I have a roof over my head and food in my belly." An employee's thermostat is set to "at least I have a **job**, and a roof over my head and food in my belly." The thermostat of a professional (doctor, lawyer, et cetera) is set to "At least I went to school and got a **good job** and have a good suburban roof over my head and quality food in my belly."

The thermostats of people like Warren Buffett (Berkshire Hathaway) Bill Gates (Microsoft) and Jeff Bezos (Amazon) are set to "be the best at what I do and take over the world! Mua ha ha ha ha!"

We humans will not fight any declines in our lives unless the decline brings us below the setting of our own thermostat (our minimum standard).

For example, Amazon profited $11.2 billion in 2018. If they "only" profited $10 billion this year, Jeff Bezos would kick his creativity into high gear, because this lowered profitability would threaten to bring him below *his* minimum standard of being the best and taking over the world. Mua ha ha ha ha!

Now, if you were the CEO of Amazon and your thermostat was set to "at least I have a roof over my head and food in my belly," you would neither fight to boost profitability, nor utilize your maximum creativity until profits dropped low enough to force Amazon to close its doors.

Why? Because dropping to $10 billion in profit from $11.2 billion would not be enough of a drop to threaten the roof over your head or the food in your belly. Even for the professional, this drop would not threaten his or her minimum standard, either, considering there is a lot of room to fall between $11.2 billion and the income the skilled professional can earn.

The married man or woman who cheats, but does not want to, has his or her thermostat set to a low temperature. Since that person's minimum standard is "as long as I don't get caught," or, "as long as the other person stays," they will cheat every now and then, until they choose to raise the setting on their own thermostat. Nothing else will stop the deceit, not even being berated by their spouse, the church, society, their parents, or members of the opposite sex. Feeling bad about hurting the other person with one's actions is not enough to stop it, either.

Hatred or disgust with your current financial situation is not enough to get you off welfare or push you to the higher ranks of your employer if you do not raise your minimum standard, the least you will accept.

Even complaining, or "telling it like it is," or "giving people a piece of your mind," with profanity (e.g., "I'm sick and tired of this s---! I need to start my own f----ing business!") won't do jacks hit, even though many people swear as if swearing and being angry will change their situation for the better.

The rich getting richer is taking money and opportunities away from everyone else. That is true! In the game of Monopoly, that is. You see, in the game of Monopoly, the monetary supply is limited to what Hasbro printed up and placed in the box.

However, the real economy does not work like that. Monetary supply is expanded whenever someone takes out institutional debt, and reduced as someone pays down their institutional debt, not to be confused with borrowing $5,000 from Uncle Jeff's bank account or $50,000 from the mafia.

Quantitative easing (QE) is an accounting trick in which the government creates new money out of thin air to purchase assets from financial institutions to increase liquidity, so banks can lawfully write more loans and spur economic activity. This pretzel logic causes less inflation of a nation's currency than if the government provided every citizen with a universal basic income.

QE is totally different from "printing money." The government only *prints* new money to replace old physical money, not to increase the monetary supply. Quantitative easing is directly responsible for much, much less new money in the economy than banks writing loans.

A bank can write in loans about as much money as it has on deposit. According to the Bank of England (the UK's central bank), a bank may even write more in loans than money it has on deposit, depending on monetary policy and the demand for loan products at the time. Check out *Money Creation in the Modern Economy* (2014) on the Bank of England's website.

When you borrow money to buy a car, the bank makes money out of thin air "at the stroke of bankers' pens" (Tobin 1963), giving you $25,000 to pay a car dealer. With that $25,000, the dealer pays the salesperson's commission, pockets any fees included in that price, and recovers the invoice amount he paid to the manufacturer.

All you have to do is sign your life away in an agreement to pay the money back over time, plus interest. This is how banks stay open. On a bank's profit and loss sheet, deposits are liabilities and outstanding loans are assets.

Your debt stimulated the economy by putting bill/spending money in the salesperson's pocket and giving the dealer some money to purchase another car to sell, keeping the assembly line workers employed. And the steel makers. And the dashboard makers. And the tire makers. And the railroad employees. And the truckers. And the list goes on.

Construction loans and home mortgages stimulate the economy in the same way!

Imagine if citizens and politicians in poor countries knew this. Instead of such citizens risking life and limb to work crummy jobs in America and send money back home from our debt-and-spending machine, poor countries would make their own debt-and-spending machines in the following ways:

Allow property developers to collectively borrow billions of dollars to pay good salaries to construction workers and purchase locally-grown timber to build nice homes. The construction workers spend their paychecks into the economy, thereby creating better-paying jobs, as well as more prosperity among entrepreneurs.

Everyone purchases more late-model automobiles, because they now have a big enough salary to qualify for auto loans. These loans pay the salaries of car salespeople, who earn enough money to qualify for a mortgage.

With more people qualifying for car loans, the big automakers can profitably operate factories in such nations, creating jobs that pay enough money to allow more people to qualify for a mortgage.

The surge in new homeowners gives the banks more confidence to give developers more money to develop more subdivisions. And more shopping malls, too, since most homeowners have enough disposable income to spend at a mall. This spending of disposable income will create part-time work opportunities for young people, thereby keeping them out of trouble.

A Discussion About Life and Work

This extra money floating in the economy would allow the governments of these nations to collect more tax revenue, thereby allowing them to pay politicians and police officers a livable wage, reducing corruption.

All of this is what people meant when they said China grew its economy by "spurring domestic consumerism."

If such nations follow China's lead, a sort of controlled capitalism, poor nations could become safer, more prosperous places to live. And no longer be poor, by the way.

They do not need much in the way of natural resources. Just look at Japan, where petroleum, iron, and precious metals are practically nonexistent.

With every nation having its own debt-and-spending machine, the nations of the world would need to agree upon controlled debt-default supercycles. It would crush the world economy if the Chinese and the Americans defaulted on their debts (public and/or private) at the same time. Or, worse yet, if half the world's nations defaulted on their debts or restructured their debts at the same time.

Furthermore, it would be imperative to recycle minerals such as phosphorus from landfills and municipal water sources (raw sewage and purified) so food and other agricultural goods will remain affordable for everyone in a world where every nation has its own debt-and-spending machine.

The rich get richer and the poor get poorer. Not true. The rich <u>minded</u> get richer, and the poor <u>minded</u> get poorer. Very few of the richest Americans in history inherited anything. One was John Pierpont (JP) Morgan, who inherited Junius Morgan's banking empire, circa 1890. Did you know that, according to *Forbes*, nearly 70% of the wealthiest 400 Americans did not inherit any of their wealth? These individuals received a Forbes Self-Made Score of a six or greater.

After the magazine created the scoring system, they retroactively applied it to the 1984 Forbes 400 list and found less than half the people on that list were self-made. Since then, the percentage of super-wealthy Americans who did not inherit anything has skyrocketed by about twenty percentage points.

Cornelius Vanderbilt is the third-richest American in history (his wealth as a share of the US economy at the time), yet his descendants spent all his money

27

in just three generations! They were poor minded. They were moneyed poor people, so to speak, much like lottery winners, and many athletes and celebrities. Well, save for Gloria Vanderbilt and her son Anderson Cooper, who were born, ironically, after most of the money had been wasted.

John Paul DeJoria (Paul Mitchell hair care, Patrón Tequila), Tyler Perry, Sylvester Stallone, Chris Gardner (portrayed in *The Pursuit of Happyness*), and Steve Harvey were homeless and became very wealthy. They are rich minded. Despite the very real risk of failure in what they were doing, they endured homelessness until they became good at what they wanted to accomplish.

Most of us, myself included, would be so hellbent on rectifying our homelessness situation, we would pump all our energy into finding (and keeping) a job or two, saving every penny, and looking for an apartment. Hey, I was homeless as a kid. That's my excuse, and I'm sticking to it.

Anyway, we would put our dreams on the back burner until our living situation improved. These guys, however, put their living situation on the back burner until their dreams improved—by becoming reality.

Chris Gardner's son was just a baby when Chris was homeless; the producers of *The Pursuit of Happyness* made the son's character older for the sake of dialog in the movie, according to Chris Gardner.

These men and other people like them wanted to accomplish their dreams so badly, they couldn't care less whether the light at the end of the tunnel was just a train or if it was actually sunlight. When you want something that is a part of your heart and soul, on a deeper level than survival and provisions, you are much more willing to give up the provisions so you can pour every crumb of your being and your energy into perfecting your craft and becoming acquainted with the right people.

Some people are born into this state. Others evolve into this state as a result of their evolving worldview, based on how they feel about certain victories, events, circumstances, situations, and injustices they have witnessed over the years.

When you are in this state, doing without the provisions does not feel quite so painful, or like such a waste of your life and time as it looks from the outside. This is true as long as you are improving your craft and not just "growing your

A Discussion About Life and Work

audience and reaching more people," but rather, you are connecting with a growing number of people who did not know how badly they were missing what you had to offer (products, skills, entertainment, et cetera) until you showed up.

This is despite the social stigma and brutal discomfort of being homeless in a developed nation.

Steve Harvey slept in his car for three years as he traveled across America performing stand-up routines, only earning about $5,000 his third year. This was in the early 1990s, and he had a wife and kids at home. Five grand a year was a part-time, minimum-wage job, even back then.

Growing your audience and reaching more people can allow you to have a profitable side hustle, or a profitable (small) business, unless you have many tens of millions of dollars of financial backing to reach millions of people.

On the other hand, connecting with a growing number of people who did not know how badly they were missing what you had to offer (products, skills, entertainment, et cetera) until you showed up has made many superstars and billionaires.

The right path to choose simply depends on what you want, and why.

Having a bigger audience is simply less inspiring, for some people who achieve high levels of success, than connecting with people and giving them something that can improve the recipient's life or work or entertain them.

Did you know Sly Stallone accepted just $35,000 to star in *Rocky* (1976), after the production company had offered him over $300,000 to *not act* in the movie he wrote? He was practically homeless! Three hundred grand in 1976 would be like millions of dollars today!

Off the top of your head, count how many rich, famous screenwriters you know of. Next, count how many rich, famous actors you know of. Now you see why Sylvester happily accepted $35,000 to *act* in the movie, as opposed to the $300,000 he was offered to just be the screenwriter.

Did you also know that most stock market gains under President Obama went into the pockets of the wealthy, in part, because most of us were too afraid of investing and losing it all again, like in 2008? I'm not sure what you were doing in 2008-09, but that is when most stock market investments and houses lost about half of their value in a few months. (Warren Buffett remained very wealthy, however, in spite of his net worth being based primarily on stocks.)

Sure, the rich always have more money *to* invest anyway, but that is not the main reason for the disproportionate gains, either.

You see, the rich realized that the only things that will completely crush the economy and the system of banking and finance as we know it are fire and brimstone raining from the sky, along with other apocalyptic terrors. That is why they bought stocks of *good companies* at rock-bottom prices, despite the very real risk of a double-dip recession. They reaped the benefits when President Obama put his $787-billion stimulus plan into action on the heels of President Bush's $700-billion cash infusion into the big banks.

Conservative Republican, Rich or well off. Liberal Democrat, Poor or on Welfare. Not true. Political views are not the root cause of poverty and inequality. Even though there are many wealthy, powerful conservative Republicans, the Republican-dominated Southern states have lower per capita earnings and higher poverty rates than the predominantly-Democrat Northeastern states, according to data from the US Census Bureau.

Your passion, effort, and energy are being wasted on the wrong thing if you are competing with immigrants for *low-wage jobs*. Between 2000 and 2010, the sources of cuts to these types of American jobs were automation (over 85%), and offshoring (less than 15%), according to various sources. This includes a report from Ball State University, entitled *The Myth and the Reality of Manufacturing in America*, which uses manufacturing data from the US Census Bureau.

Instead of stressing over low-paying jobs, devote your life to either being a creator of such jobs, or competing with *highly-educated* immigrants for jobs actually worth fighting over! Fight for $15,000 per month, not $15 per hour.

Bad credit is a choice, made subconsciously. "I work hard, I deserve this. I work hard, I deserve that. All the crap I put up with on this job." Growing up deprived worsens these sentiments especially when you hate your job, or you do it just to make money and provide. If you do something just for the money, you will generally feel overworked and underpaid, *no matter how much it pays.*

So, how does this translate into bad credit? If you get no pleasure from the work itself or what it provides outside of money, the only way to derive pleasure from it is to spend your earnings. All your earnings. Then, when you are out of earnings, go into as much debt as you are comfortable with. This is why financial planners like Suze Orman tell us to get more pleasure from saving than from spending.

Most of us are not trying to keep up with the Joneses. Rather, we are merely purchasing the biggest lifestyle we can, between our income and what creditors are willing to lend us. Some welfare recipients are in the same boat.

What do you truly believe about blacks and wealth? About whites and wealth? Whatever you truly believe about the two will shape your actions, and in turn, your reality. If you really and truly believe deep in your heart that "black folks can't have nothing, this is a white man's world; I'm just living in it," or, "Black equals foot on your neck, rough neighborhoods, people throwing trash out their cars," and <u>you happen to be black</u>...then guess what?

If you do somehow become successful or land a high-paying job, your subconscious mind will nudge success out of your life with subtle actions.

And worse yet, since your actions will be *subtle*, the cause will disguise itself in your mind as something many black people *actually deal with*, such as racism and less access to starting capital from banks and venture capitalists. Or it might disguise itself as discontent with the high-paying job, or your business' customers and employees making you crazy, or the economy slowing down and taking your business with it.

These negative views are reinforced by TV, music, cinema, the news, and statistics. There are many movies that demonize wealth, while making the actors, producers, and studios involved even wealthier. Newscasters earn lots of money to tell people how bad the economy is, or how hard it is for a poor person to change their circumstances. Growing up in a poor neighborhood and listening to poor elders and single parents can also reinforce these deep-seated beliefs. I personally have spent over a decade actively working to unbelieve these things myself.

Joblessness among blacks is twice what it is for whites, and poverty is three times what it is for whites. People who are born into poverty have a 42% chance of dying in poverty. These stats are in America, by the way. You should be worried. That is, if you are going to just work jobs the rest of your career. Otherwise,

Just ignore the statistics and commit to who you want to be, where you want to go in life, and the mark you want to leave. If we all do this, the statistics will change over time because the people behind them will have changed.

Watch *The Men Who Built America* (2012), from a perspective without regards to race/class/gender or color. If a person continues to focus on how he or she is different from their idea of rich people, they will continue to be different from rich people where it counts: in the wallet.

Followers (employees) are paid by the hour. Leaders are paid based on performance. In most companies, entry-level employees and their immediate supervisors are paid hourly. Higher-level supervisors are paid a salary, plus a bonus based on performance. And therein lies the centuries-old battle between management and labor. The few who are paid based on performance are trying to wrench performance out of the many whose pay remains the same, irrespective of performance! "They're still going to pay me the same $11 an hour. I ain't killing myself for these people."

Receiving a $0.50-per-hour raise annually for working hard and showing great work ethic in an entry-level position is some incentive but not on par with bonuses paid to management. Worse yet, some of this incentive is diminished by the fact that even people who do as little as possible or who don't want to "kill themselves" in an entry-level position may still receive a $0.10 or $0.25 raise!

It appears companies do this to 1) Force more people into the leadership pipeline to replace high-level leaders who retire; and 2) Avoid needing to pay too much attention to individual performance of employees outside of leadership, and just pay them based on the <u>average</u> productivity for the whole plant, per employee, keeping things simple.

Every leader is paid based on performance, whether he or she is the CEO of a publicly-traded company, or the owner of a local shop. It is a classic case of risk versus reward. Hourly employees don't earn much, but what they do earn is more secure, and they can file for unemployment. If a leader performs well, he or she can pay oneself well. If not, this person cannot turn to unions or unemployment benefits.

Leader is a person, not a job title or a position within a company.

"Management is the development of people, not the direction of things." – Bob Proctor

Over the years, I have noticed that subordinates take after their leaders. Good leaders can improve lazy people to an extent. Good leaders bring out the best in good employees. Good leaders make everyone more knowledgeable and coherent.

Lazy leaders can make good workers stop going the extra mile and become less passionate or enthusiastic about the job. Leaders who don't give a you-know-what can make good employees stop caring so much and pay less attention to details.

Moreover, the dominant attitudes and behaviors of many lower- and mid-level managers usually reflect those in the managers at the top.

For example, if the people at the top express empathy, the lower-level managers tend to be the same way. If the top leaders are condescending jerks, the ones below them are more likely to be that way, too. If the leaders at the top are concerned with looking good as opposed to fixing issues (such as assembly lines running out of parts for production multiple times a day), the lower-level leaders tend to make their employees "look busy" as much as possible, so they themselves may look good for the higher ups.

Like promotes like. What kind of culture and attitudes do you want in your company? It has to look after the employees, profitability, and customer satisfaction. The answer to that question dictates the type of leader you should strive to become.

What do you need to sacrifice in order to become successful? We hear lots of talk about hard work and sacrifice, but what exactly should we sacrifice? These discussions usually center around women, parties, drugs, booze, procrastination, and sometimes beauty sleep. Guess what? These are the easy sacrifices.

So, what is the most difficult sacrifice we need to make in order to become successful? Our beliefs.

The easy sacrifices feel difficult when you have not yet sacrificed your current beliefs about **people like you, under your circumstances**.

Beliefs are not to be confused with knowledge and hypothetical situations. You can know (possess knowledge) that you are capable of just about anything, but are you living your life by that knowledge? Many of us say we *believe* anything is possible, when we actually *hope* things just "get better" on their own, perhaps by God working a miracle.

We make our decisions, and in turn, live our lives based on our beliefs, not mere knowledge. It takes lots of concentrated effort, in many cases, years, to force your beliefs to emulate your knowledge. Many people's beliefs do not match their knowledge. You see, our deepest beliefs are the wagonmaster of our lives; women, parties, drugs, and *knowledge* are not.

The US tax code is unfair, but that is not the root cause of poverty or wealth inequality.

Presidential candidate Willard "Mitt" Romney made news in 2012 for "earning" $20 million in capital gains for 2011 and only paying an effective tax rate of about 14%. Let us assume the government changed the tax code so anyone with a gross annual income of $50,000 or less paid no taxes, not even state income taxes or FICA for Medicare and Social Security. Meanwhile, the big shots paid a 95% tax rate, regardless of the source of their income.

So, someone earning $9.75 per hour would keep all his or her $20,000 per year. Meanwhile, Mitt with his $20 million would have to pay 95% to the government, or $19 million. Even after that tax rape, he would still be left with...ONE MILLION DOLLARS!

Even with this tax schedule that is more fair to the average worker, the person earning $9.75 per hour would still need to **work for 50 years** to go out and earn what Mitt Romney sat back and netted in capital gains in **just one year.** Someone earning $50,000 per year would still have to **work for 20 years** to match Romney's after-tax income for **just one year.**

Focus on how you can *best* serve enough people to earn $20 million worth of their business each year. Who will you have to become? What characteristics should your employees possess?

Remember, if you want something done right, you've got to do it yourself. If you want it done right on a large scale, you've got to educate and develop the right people and incentivize them to do it.

The economy *is* debt and spending. That's why there are so many mortgage and credit card ads. Did you know that, according to the Federal Reserve Bank of St. Louis, nearly 70% of the economy is based on spending? According to the National Retail Federation, about one-fifth of that spending takes place during the holiday season of November and December.

The Christmas ads used to start after Thanksgiving. However, since the Great Recession of 2008-09, they now start around Halloween. The rush is so large, manufacturing, transportation, and logistics companies ramp up in September and do not slow down until about December 22. The holidays are not so much about God and family but more about that which is emblazoned with "In God We Trust."

If people quit spending money they don't have on things they don't need, the economy would tank. Sorry, Dave Ramsey. Sorry, Suze Orman.

However, if people do start saving more money and getting into less debt, *en masse*, people might become creative and shape a new economy that allows us to keep modern conveniences, such as electricity and McMansions, without being propped up with increasing consumer debt.

Remember 2007-10? Many experts told us the Great Recession was caused by consumers being overextended with debts. It was actually caused by companies doing everything to cut jobs and labor expenses starting in 2002-03, which slowed down the labor market. This eventually fed on itself because people who are laid off cannot pay their bills, spend money, and stimulate the economy very well with welfare checks and unemployment benefits.

Moreover, real-estate fraud and predatory lending practices pushed the cost of housing through the roof; and the price of energy was artificially inflated, even as the economy slowed down in late 2006. Remember $4.50-a-gallon gas in 2008, anyone? (It was $5.50 per gallon for full service.)

Then, after all of this, in 2010-11, the big companies used the employer's market (fewer jobs, slashed wages, high unemployment, and higher minimum job qualifications) they helped create as an excuse to be slow to hire people after the worst of the recession had passed, even as they had a record $2 trillion of cash reserves between them! This figure is according to the *WSJ* article, entitled "Companies Cling to Cash. Coffers Swell to 51-Year High as Cautious Firms Put Off Investing in Growth."

Is that the truth, or neoliberal hyperbole? You decide.

Anyway, debt and spending were the "official" culprits, but President Bush borrowed $700 billion and gave it to the big banks so they could write loans? And after that, President Obama borrowed $787 billion for his stimulus plan to encourage people to buy houses and new cars by going into debt and spending money they don't have? Well, how else? Most people do not have $150,000 for a house or $20,000 for a new car lying around collecting dust, especially after their 401(k)'s and home equity were vaporized in 2008.

The Republican party was pushing for a balanced budget and reduced federal spending but not to eliminate the need to borrow money. No, no. They pushed for this to prove to credit rating agencies (like Moody's, not Experian or Equifax) that Uncle Sam can pay his bills so as to keep America's credit rating high, so the government could borrow money at lower interest rates? Hey, the Republicans overspend, too, just on different things from the Democrats.

Don't worry, though. The same skills that make people wealthy in the monetary system can be applied to attain success in any system of trade. These skills are leadership, honesty and integrity, taking risks most people will not take, and giving people the best products and services with the best attitude.

Help! I Don't Know My Passion!

If you don't know your passion, the path to finding it is simple: identify what you like to do, you can effortlessly perform at a high level, and how you can use it to fulfill the needs and wants of others or solve their problems.

Do not expect a business or career based on your passion to make you *happy*, per se. Working with people and earning money, even doing something you love, still has the psychological rigors of work and business; only your *perception* of them will be a bit muted.

If you do not know what you are good at, have no fear. Simply work various jobs for about fifteen years, and become great at each job, spending at least two years at each one. Work in customer service positions. Working in a restaurant *kitchen* does not count; you have to interact with customers directly, be it face to face or over the phone. Work manual labor positions in warehouses and factories. Mix it up over time.

This will give you enough experiences to allow you to clearly see problems you are good at solving and like to solve. You will get to learn from people of many different ages and nationalities. You get to experience well-run companies, and those not run so well.

Best of all, you get to see how different personalities and departments within a business must work together to keep the business open. You want your own company someday, right?

Fifteen years? WTF? Here's the deal: When you are no longer terrified of becoming the next generation of grumbly old people who hate their jobs, you will think much more clearly and make better decisions. You will also learn how to embrace the suck, as they say in the military, and be better prepared intellectually and emotionally to handle the rigors of successfully following your passion as a career or business.

You will reap the greatest benefit if you also cut back your living expenses so you can try and fail at various businesses within those fifteen years.

"That sounds like too much," I hear you say. "I want to have a life; I want to have fun, live a little. What if it never goes anywhere and I just end up wasting my life and my money?"

Look, if you're that frickin' terrified of making mistakes or being viewed as a screw-up by family, friends, and associates, you should just work jobs to earn money; pursue your passion as a hobby instead of a career; and become an entrepreneur in the sense of having a side hustle to earn extra money, as opposed to starting a full-fledged business or becoming a celebrity and putting your eggs in such a risky basket.

If money and creature comforts are more important to you, make those things primary, and your passion secondary.

It's okay, even in this time when *entrepreneur* is such a sexy word!

However, if there is a cat in your bag that you feel absolutely needs to get out, maybe even a divinely-ordained cat, you've got to make the cat far more important than saving face, or avoiding suffering and mistakes. Meow!

Whatever you do, just get out of the no-man's land of nes, yo, maybe. We stay in this no-man's land because, let's face it, we want all the pleasure each path can provide and none of the pain. We want the income security of an employee or welfare recipient, while enjoying the wealth and perceived freedom of a successful business owner.

Get out of no-man's land, and embrace the pain of whichever path you choose, while focusing on the positives of your chosen path. By trying to avoid one type of pain, we only suffer a different type of pain. I'll admit, it took a month of suffering the physical pain and temporary paralysis of the West Nile Virus to make me much less afraid of pain, in all its forms and shapes. It also made me realize that "tired" or "can't" are just softer ways of saying "won't" or "don't want to."

The truth is, it takes the average person about a decade of constantly trying and failing at business in order to develop what it takes intellectually and emotionally to run a business. No six-month or one-year breaks between failures.

If you take too much time off between failures, you will never clearly see your unique pain points that cause you to throw in the towel. The only way to overcome them *is to see them clearly*. That way, it becomes more difficult to brush off your pain points as the economy going south, people just not buying your products, or your successful competitors just getting lucky.

You may as well work a job and get better at business simultaneously. If you try to start a business when your ducks are in a row, however, it could easily take a quarter of a century, not just fifteen years, of working for you to succeed in business.

That's if you don't feel as though you're *too old* to devote your life to starting a business, as opposed to merely trying your hand at business, *after* fifteen to twenty-five years of working.

Many people do feel as though they are *too old* by this point, especially if they are over fifty years of age, or as young as thirty-five if they started a family in their twenties. Deep down, we know it is safer and less emotionally draining to just stick with the tried-and-true method of working jobs and distracting ourselves with vacations and adult beverages until retirement age.

Consequently, young people feel they are too young to get into business. Then, when they do grow into their thirties and forties, they feel as though they are too busy with the responsibilities of raising a family and maintaining a marriage and a career; then, when fifty rolls around, they feel as though they are too old.

Again, the average person has not developed what it takes to be successful in business unless he or she has continued to wholeheartedly work at business long after running out of money, patience, and sanity, until finally achieving success. Most people stop after running out of money, and a few stop after running out of patience. It is best to run out of all three of these things before you turn forty, as you will have more time to recover when you are relatively young and less fearful.

My Issue with The Secret

Although the guests in the film spoke the truth, the cinematography was much too whimsical. Well, okay, maybe the guy who talked about visualizing checks in the mail and getting them was also a bit too whimsical as well.

The movie showed people imagining things, then the Universe (God) forking it over like a genie. For instance, the woman who visualized the expensive necklace could have been shown doing a better job at work, being more engaged with customers and co-workers, and landing a series of promotions.

Instead, the film showed her wealthy husband or boyfriend handing her the expensive necklace.

Toward the end of the movie, the Universe was portrayed as a genie saying, "Your wish is my command."

Truth is, the Universe will *tell* you how to get what you want. The problem is most of us don't like the steps the Universe is telling us to take. They require us to not just "work hard," but to do so in a *new direction*. Not an unethical direction, just a new one.

So, instead of following those steps, we just keep arguing back and forth with the Universe, trying to get it to just fork over what we want, without us making any drastic changes on our part.

Basically, we passionately hope and pray for massive gains by working even harder in the same *old direction*.

The steps to success are easy *to do* but not easy *on you*.

Furthermore, when the movie was heavily hyped in 2006, several references were made to the million-dollar check Jim Carrey wrote himself, post-dated

November 1995. This, coincidentally, was the time *$10 million* were deposited into his bank account for acting in *Dumb and Dumber* the year before.

Many people in 2006 and '07 (myself included, I'll admit, before I was enlightened) wrote outrageous post-dated checks to themselves, after knowing Jim Carrey received ten times the money he "asked the Universe to give him."

The truth is this was a sixteen-year journey to $10 million. He dropped out of high school in 1978 to help his family financially. In 1979 he moved to Los Angeles and pursued comedy full time.

According to mathematics, 1979 through 1995 is sixteen years of rolling with the punches as a struggling stand-up comedian, constantly improving his craft, being the "white comic" on *In Living Color* from 1990-94, starring in three movies in 1994, and finally being paid the following year.

Are you that committed to reaching your goals, even with the ever-present risk of failure? I hope so.

Don't Call Yourself an Entrepreneur

You know how many social-media biographies say *entrepreneur*? Too many. I've asked people face to face what they do, and some just say, "I'm an entrepreneur." During the 2008 economic meltdown, many of us took solace in the idea of being an entrepreneur because we saw it as a hedge against the terrible labor market, which shed over eight million American jobs in a matter of months.

"I don't need no stinkin' job. Humph! I'll just be an entrepreneur, be my own boss, work for myself."

There were more voices in the media than ever telling people to follow their passion, chase their dreams and become an entrepreneur. This message sells a lot of seminar tickets during recessions.

Critically-acclaimed television shows about business and entrepreneurship, such as *Shark Tank* (2009) and *Undercover Boss* (2009), debuted around that time. The opening to early episodes of *Undercover Boss* even mentioned the discontent of America's middle class as out-of-touch corporate executives made more money than ever during a time of record unemployment.

Instead of calling yourself an entrepreneur, or saying you're "on your grind," just tell people specifically what you do for work. Are you a plumber? An accountant? A mobile mechanic?

If you call yourself a producer, do you actively build relationships with nightclub owners, radio disc jockeys, and music-hall personnel to promote artists and their music? Do you bring together different trades and talents in the music industry for your projects? Do you oversee the production of vocals and music of several other artists? With so many people on social media aggrandizing their work and accomplishments, it is best to just tell people specifically what you do; there are enough "CEOs, *entrepreneurs*, and producers" as it is.

Emotional Detachment Is a Good Thing

Until you get over the hump. This is not to be misconstrued as taking solace in alcohol and other vices. Rather, you may have to make the difficult decision to keep people you love and care about a safe distance away as you go through your metamorphosis.

The truth is, the people with whom we are closest, though meaning well, are the ones who gave us the worldview and perception of self that have prevented us from becoming who we want to be thus far. We will continue living small lives trying to maintain their favor by avoiding mistakes. You can usually stay in touch, but at the same time, they will subconsciously do and say things to try to make you stay the same as you are today. Why? If you stay the same, others do not have to worry about you outgrowing them or leaving them permanently.

More importantly, they never have to fully come to grips with the fact they never pushed themselves to *fully* undergo the metamorphosis they should have undergone themselves to become the person they wanted to become.

For instance, if you are trying to lose weight, your lover may buy more candy for you, and take you out to dinner more often. Some will go so far as to tell you things such as, "Oh, you've exercised enough this week," or mock your efforts.

Once you have become who you need to be, you are 100% firm in your new way of thinking and being, and you accomplished what you set out to accomplish, you can then rebuild *certain* relationships.

The emotional and psychological stress of growth and change and entering the unknown will take their toll on you. That is unless you start to compartmentalize certain feelings, or deflect them by viewing them as, say, scenes from an action movie. My go-to is Sarah Connor's escape from the Pescadero mental hospital in T2: Judgment Day.

Initially, you will have to force and fight to get yourself to do what you already know is necessary. Then, after about a decade of forcing and fighting and being serious about what you are trying to accomplish, you start to trust yourself enough and you have studied yourself enough to know how to loosen up and *flow* into taking the correct action without it feeling like a struggle to make yourself do it.

While it does take periodic discipline to maintain the flow, you are also far less likely to waste time on detrimental activities once you finally reach this state, even when you loosen up and relax. It usually takes gobs of discipline and fighting before you have found or created reasons in line with who you are on a much deeper level than the reasons you had when you started the journey.

People like the so-called Rebel Billionaire, Richard Branson, who are few and far between, are almost born with the ability to just flow. No forcing and fighting for ten years. He is called the Rebel Billionaire, due in part to the fact he never worked a "real job." Okay, okay, and some of his death-defying stunts. Around age fifteen, he started a magazine. When he was about twenty, a friend of his made some music Richard liked, but record labels would not distribute it.

Richard did not spend time trying to emulate the rituals and habits of successful people, nor did he go through the typical logic pattern of, "I'm too young, I don't know anybody, I don't even know where to begin." He did not waste time attempting to use success hacks. Ol' Rich likely said, "Screw it, let's do it," and just flowed into the correct sequence of actions to start a record label, the beginning of his Virgin empire. The rest of us have to fight ourselves for ten years, putting everything else on the back burner.

Hey, life ain't fair. And that's okay. Sir Richard is a rare breed. At least being a rare breed is not the only way to get what we want out of life. Rare breeds just get there faster, and that's okay, too.

How Do the Rich Get Richer?

Easy. Pick an industry. Stick with it. Get good at it, serve customers. Get better at it, serve more customers, and before it becomes too much for one person, bring on some high-quality people. Work in the trenches with them as you teach them how to serve your customers. Go out and get more customers and/or do more things for your current customers. Rinse and repeat.

And, above all else, get rid of the poisonous mindset of, "I want to have so much money, I never have to work again."

Remember, most of us hate our jobs due in part to higher-ups making decisions based on spreadsheets, conference calls, and stock prices from the comfort of their ivory towers, not even spending a few weeks a year in the trenches actually performing, as opposed to observing, the high-volume, low-skill work. Even though low-skill labor faces a fierce competitor in automation, low-skill labor is still the meat and potatoes of a company's profitability.

All of this raises two questions: 1) How do I pick a suitable industry, and 2) What about multiple streams of income?

Basically, there are two types of industries to choose from. The first type is one with an obvious demand, such as real estate or apparel. The second type is one in which the product or service can be useful, but the demand is not there, such as an automobile in 1908, or a personal computer in 1975.

Both types of industries have their own hills to climb. If there is an obvious demand (and an obvious way to make money), the industry will be overcrowded, and full of people selling "picks and shovels during a gold rush." Nursing and IT classes, anyone? Real-estate seminars?

T-shirt screen printing services?

However, if the demand or usefulness is not obvious, you have the daunting task of educating the masses. Henry Ford had to tell people something along the lines of, "While you think you want faster horses, you're wrong. You don't want faster horses; you want an automobile the common man can afford."

Get it? Af-Ford?

But, at any rate, picking one industry is crucial because, if you keep the options open, you run the <u>very</u> real risk of becoming a jack of all trades, master of none. This is because as soon as one industry becomes too emotionally draining, or puts you face to face with too many fears or *uncertainties*, you will run to another, and the entire process will begin anew.

So, pick one industry, and "stay in the fire," if you will, so as to anneal yourself and become tougher. Rich people are less afraid of failing than they are of living with the regret of going to the grave having played it safe. Also, many rich people get a rush from succeeding at something with a high possibility for failure, especially after they ran out of money multiple times and had a few brushes with foreclosure. Crazy, ain't it?

Now, for multiple streams of income. Let us revisit Andrew Carnegie, the Scottish American steel titan and second-richest American in history.

Although he picked the steel industry in his early thirties, stuck with it for about thirty years, and advocated putting all your eggs in one basket (and watching the basket), he also had multiple streams of income. He had four major streams, in fact. You see, his steel went into defense projects, skyscrapers, railroad expansion and upgrades, and more modern bridges that could carry heavier loads with fewer pylons in the ground.

Although Nigerian billionaire Aliko Dangote is involved in multiple industries, he stayed in the import/export business for twenty-five years before manufacturing cement, and about another fifteen before getting into the petroleum refining business.

Here's where most of us go wrong with *multiple streams of income*: We attempt multiple side hustles in different industries, all at the same time. Worse yet, we try to do it all by ourselves. Why do so many of us do it this way? The answer is simple: Most of us do not trust other people, and we are **obsessed** with having something to fall back on. You know the old adages. Good help is hard to find. Folks crazy these days. If you want something done right, you've got to do it yourself. Can't even trust your own family.

Many rich people have been burned by other people in business, especially in their early days. William "Devil Bill" Rockefeller Sr., John D. Rockefeller's own father, cheated young John and his brothers Frank and William Jr. in business deals. William Sr. is even quoted as saying, "I cheat my boys every chance I get. I trade with the boys and skin 'em and I just beat 'em every time I can. I want to make 'em sharp."

The rich eventually became better judges of character, better at understanding contracts, and ultimately became successful. Judging character is a skill that only gets better with practice. Once you have worked with enough lambs and enough wolves in lambs' clothing, you steadily become better at knowing the difference.

Don't allow your distrust of people to keep you poor or relegate yourself to the life of a <u>small</u> business owner who works ninety to 100 hours a week to earn an income in the <u>low</u> six figures.

Running through the fire, if you will, of becoming a better judge of character will allow you to build a great team of people, serve more customers, and in turn, become rich. Moreover, if you fall ill and spend a month in the hospital, your team will continue to run the business, and you will be able to comfortably afford any hospital bills and other medical expenses.

Basically, the rich get richer by excelling in one industry, becoming good at building a great team, and continuing to build their organizations bigger and better **<u>long after they initially become wealthy</u>**.

Pray for Riches?

In my experience, God is more Mentor than Miracle Worker when it comes to enhancing our health, wealth, love, and happiness beyond the most basic level.

In the realm of wealth and riches, I would suggest picking <u>one</u> industry based on the demand for it and your ability to do it.

Once you do this, it is time to take action as you are learning your chosen industry, not waiting until you're an expert. The longer you stick with it and aim to get good at it, the clearer will be the voice of God in the form of intuition, inclinations, and hearing the right words from people at the right time. However, if you try your hand at multiple unrelated businesses simultaneously, God will flood you out with intuition and inclinations for ALL of your businesses, simultaneously. As in more than your brain can effectively and coherently process all at once.

Let's say you're dabbling in real estate, stocks, hairdressing, and making T-shirts. Each industry can be likened to a physical location. Imagine you are driving a car with four GPS units, one for each location, active at the same time. Worse yet, each one gives directions using the same whispering voice as the others!

It is a garbled cacophony of whispering voices at every traffic signal.

And each one is right, in its own way.

With that being said, there will be times when God Himself tells you to do something that will be a painful mistake. Why? Because it is better to learn from big mistakes with a small amount of money, small staff, small customer base, and a small reputation at stake, as opposed to the other way around.

What about timing? Is there such a thing as starting too late or too soon?

Based on what I've seen, I would advise you to start right now. Wasting time and money by starting too soon and *eventually* seizing the opportunity is better than missing out on the opportunity by starting too late.

Since you ain't gonna get the timing perfect, anyhow, you might as well pick the poison of starting too early. Sure, you may have $0 in the bank and not be well connected, but paying customers have all the money you will ever need.

In the process of perfecting your idea, you can reach out to potential customers and ask for their opinion about what's right and wrong with your product or service, what they would change about it, and how much they would pay if your execution lines up with the promise.

If you can be profitable with a small volume of business, you can charge your customers first, buy raw materials, then deliver the finished product.

However, if your business needs a large amount of volume to be profitable, you must conduct more thorough market research, submit a business plan to multiple investors, and become emotionally ready to cede power, control, and equity to your investors. Try to find investors with core values similar to your own.

If they push you to grow bigger than you want, just remember that twenty investors sharing 49% of a million-dollar business will not be happy, even if it provides enough for you and your family. They want a handsome return on their money. While they are still alive, that is.

Did you know that Jeff Bezos, in 1995, had to meet with sixty different investors to raise a million dollars to start Amazon? Forty said no. About twenty gave approximately $50,000 apiece.

Perhaps the most compelling reason you should start now is that every novel idea has a maturity date. If you wait too long, God will put your big idea in someone else's head, and he or she will get it done.

As an example, in 2003, I thought of a proactive ride-control system for automobiles. Older ride-control systems merely tell the suspension how to react, after a pothole has been struck. I never told anyone, nor did I write it down. Lo, and behold! More than a decade later, Mercedes-Benz engineers create Automatic Body Control (ABC) which uses a 3D stereo camera to observe road irregularities before the car encounters them—a proactive ride-control system.

With that being said, I would advise against praying for riches but instead praying for an open heart and an open mind that are more capable of understanding and acting on God's advice. I truly believe it is easier to hear God when we stop praying for things, circumstances, and people to show up (or go away). Next, pick an industry, get good at it, listen to God, and most importantly, realize that your pain and mistakes are just as divinely ordained as your eventual success, and vice versa.

Ageism and 40-Year-Olds

Seemingly every generation gets blindsided by this phenomenon, even though it has run rampant since the 1980s. We humans tend to think, "Oh, that's not going to happen to me."

Until it does. So, here are some things you can do, regardless of your current age, to minimize the effects of ageism on your career.

The first thing one can do is actively seek a leadership role with his or her current employer and the extra responsibilities. The supply/demand ratio for entry-level employees is higher than that for low-level leadership, and astronomically higher than the supply/demand ratio for high-level leadership.

People in entry-level positions are first fired, last hired, and usually replaced with robots or young, unskilled workers who are more impressionable and willing to work for less.

Now, let's assume you've already been displaced, and you have applied all over the place. Research local employers in your field and pick one or two whose culture and growth prospects line up with your career goals. I say only one or two because the key to success is to build working relationships, not just "looking for a job." Next, find their physical address.

At certain times of day, people flood out of these places of employment to buy lunch, smoke cigarettes, and go home.

Not just any people. People who are a part of your industry. Sure, some will tell you to get lost, and many will politely tell you about the employer's jobs website. However, a few may actually be able to pull some strings if you have the necessary hard and soft skills and keep in touch, buy their lunch every now and then.

Some office towers such as Symphony Tower in midtown Atlanta, while not bearing a company logo, may still be mostly occupied by a single employer. Upon the building's opening in 2006, a single law firm, King & Spalding LLP, occupied three-fifths of the tower's office space.

There is also a soft approach: applying to lesser jobs at these places of business so as to get in where you fit in and move on from there. And of course, learning from the right people how to *properly* use Facebook and LinkedIn to market your skills, since you have likely rolled the dice on those sites already.

Do you possess enough skills and wisdom that individuals and small businesses want so badly, they will pay you to be a consultant? Although large, often publicly-traded companies shed senior employees to cut costs, many small, rapidly-growing companies could greatly benefit from a talented, highly-skilled, seasoned worker as a consultant or even a senior officer.

While such companies may pay you 40% less in salary and benefits, and give you 40% more work, this is better than the brain drain you would invariably suffer being unemployed or working at a warehouse. Trust me, I have experienced both.

Fortunately, if you put your skills and talents to the best use, you can potentially propel the small company to a point in a few years where you can negotiate a better compensation package without hurting the company budget.

Now that you know how the story goes, it is time to look beyond earning a paycheck. Do not just occupy a leadership position and "make more money than some grunt or some pencil pusher"; rather, increase your value to your organization and your industry. Network outside of your comfort zone more aggressively and creatively, with the intention of helping your connections become richer as well.

I WANT YOU TO SUCCEED. DO YOU?

Our lives are piloted by what we deeply and truly believe about **people like us, under our circumstances**. I emphasize deeply because we all *superficially* and truly believe that anything is possible.

I mean, it happened for Oprah, Bill Gates, and the Obamas, to name a few.

If you want it to happen for you, start by telling yourself, "I'm going to do it, whether I like it or not," on a daily basis. Say it aloud every so often.

You will also need to get some painful emotions and baggage from the past off your chest (including mommy and daddy issues) by facing it, working through it, and coming out on the other side realizing you are still alive and stronger than you previously thought.

Seemingly unrelated to the topic at hand but critical to breaking the chains that hold you back from success nonetheless.

So, why is it "whether I like it or not" as opposed to "whether they like it or not"? Here's the thing: If you've been poor your whole life, you don't even know if you will enjoy being rich and staying rich, much less the emotionally-draining process to get there. The same thing goes for losing lots of weight and keeping it off. Again, if you have been overweight your whole life, you don't know if you will enjoy being thin after changing your entire lifestyle to get there.

And one more thing: even if "they" are somehow responsible for your demise, "they" will not pull you out unless it will help *them*, not you.

You can also repeat the phrase to yourself in the second person as, for example, "Look, Mitchell, you are going to do this, whether you like it or not." Believe that you are worthy of it because God put you on earth. Now, a word of caution: be sure to require yourself to do it in a legal, honest, ethical fashion.

I say this because once you start talking to yourself in this way, every day, your mind will look for what it believes is the most economical way to achieve success.

Many of us, consciously or unconsciously, believe that the most economical route to financial success is to do something crooked to stockpile cash, then use that cash to go legit. This belief is further reinforced by several decades of shows and movies about people laundering dirty money.

Worse yet, when people become successful in an honest manner, they typically gloss over the specifics with platitudes, such as hard work, dedication, grit, determination, commitment, and sacrifice.

The problem with that is most people take the platitudes at face value and believe them to mean "spend eighty hours a week working two crummy jobs, or go to college, get some letters behind your name and *make more money*," as opposed to leading people and becoming an indispensable member of the industry or organization for which you work, from the vantage point of customers, the employer, and most of your co-workers.

Try putting more focus on the legal aspects first. While religion can serve as a moral compass, a hyper focus on certain parables about money and vanity may hit the pause button on journeys of wealth building or weight loss, or trigger a reversal of fortune once you accomplish these things.

God doesn't want us to be poor and unhappy; he just doesn't want us stepping on the toes of others or using trickery to achieve our earthly desires. Job was rich.

I say this because I know some of you, who have not read a Bible or a Qur'an in twenty years, will suddenly crack one open so you can twist the words of God and use them to stay stuck in your current situation, short of God handing you a miracle of biblical proportions.

So, along with learning everything you can about what you are trying to do and speaking with experts, just stay on the side of laws and ethics, and tell yourself (with conviction) you are going to do it, whether you like it or not.

Does It Take Money to Make Money?

We will review three ways in which various companies, entrepreneurs, and *hustlas* have used paying customers as a source of start-up capital.

1. The customer buys the raw materials, then you bill them for labor. Now, I'm sure you know someone like Nae in apartment 4C who does hair.
2. Customers pay the full purchase price up front, and you provide them with a lead time, say, ten days. This gives you enough time to source materials, assemble the finished product, and ship it to the customer. Custom cabinetry, anyone?
3. Charge a purchase price that will make your company profitable at its current scale, and request a down payment before commencing work. Once you collect enough down payments to build one unit (including parts, labor, insurance, tool rental, fuel, delivery, et cetera) you can build one unit, then demand the remainder of the purchase price from the first depositor. Now, you will have the profit from the sale of the first unit, plus the remaining deposits. You can then use this cycle of profits and remaining deposits to build and deliver the second and subsequent units in a stepwise manner. Sounds like a good way to *Kickstarter* your business to me (pun intended). What if the first customer cannot pay on time?

Does It Take Money to Make Money?

Make your product easy to modify. That way, one customer will not hold up your entire business if he or she is unable to pay.

Some of you are thinking, "Yeah, Mitchell, that *sounds* great, but how do I get the customers?"

Well, first, where do your potential customers spend their free time? For instance, if you are launching a fashion brand, your customers will likely spend time at apparel stores, barbershops, and salons. Talk to these people, write down their wants, needs, and opinions. You can also talk to the business owners and forge alliances with them. Talk to celebrities, famous and aspiring alike.

Now, if your potential customers don't get out much, what magazines do they read? If your product is very compelling (like Tesla automobiles in 2010), the editor may write an article about your business, if you pick up the phone and call them until they respond. People who have succeeded in this way have made many phone calls to the same editor over a period of months, on top of having a very compelling product or service. Better than paying big money to advertise in such magazines.

Don't care for magazines? Call up local affiliate stations for the major networks, such as NBC 4 New York, FOX 2 Detroit, et cetera. Again, if your product or service is very compelling, they may run a news story.

As for blogs and social media, find posts relevant to your industry. Second, write comments relevant to the post and show your knowledge or skill in that area without bashing the author of the post. Furthermore, stay away from calls to action when commenting on someone else's post. You could mention something the likes of "twenty years' experience" somewhere in your post, however.

Calls to action in the comments seem very spammy or robotic and may be flagged as such. A social-media page name such as "Bob's Kustom Karz" coupled with a display of your knowledge is an understated call to action, without being spammy. This combination tells fellow gearheads, "This guy named Bob not only builds custom cars; he also knows what he is talking about."

For your own page, I would suggest the following:

Use your biographical section for contact info and hard calls to action, while using your posts to invite questions, comments, and feedback. Visually-appealing pictures and proper spelling and usage of words will showcase your attention to detail. If most of your business is local you can add a few location tags; if you own an e-commerce business, location hashtags will be an unnecessary distraction.

That's all fine and good, but what if I need half a million dollars for a production run, warehouse rental, buying tools, hiring full-time labor, maybe building a website, and hiring some security guards?

First, build a working mock-up from cheap parts from Amazon, Walmart, and Lowe's. Next, focus-group the heck out of such mock-ups and live-stream the meetings to your social-media audience. You can host focus group meetings at beautiful public parks, your home, et cetera. If you live in the American South, be mindful of the afternoon downpours that materialize from nowhere every July and August. Well, those are always good ideas, anyway, regardless of how much money you *think* your business needs. Those options are cheaper than hiring an engineering firm and a marketing firm or renting a conference room.

You should not borrow or spend great sums of money prior to thoroughly proving your concept.

Though no one likes to be criticized, knowing what customers like about your product, the changes they would make, and how much they will pay if your execution meets or exceeds their expectations is crucial for your success. Once you know what they will pay, you can research and experiment with ways to profitably meet the customers' demands.

Another thing: Keep Napoleon Hill's QQS formula in mind. This stands for the quality and quantity of service you render, and the spirit in which you render it. If your spirit or attitude is bad, you can "sir" or "ma'am" people all you want, but your poor spirit will drag down a person's opinion of you and your operation.

Don't allow a difficult customer or personal circumstances to spill over into your interactions with other people.

As for the hypothetical half a million dollars, you can attend trade shows, flea markets/swap meets and scour social media for your target audience (not racking up random followers and likes) to reach 10,000 customers who will deposit $50 each, or 50,000 people who will deposit $10 each, depending on what you are offering for sale. Just be 100% honest with your depositors, from the beginning, about how you will use their money. Furthermore, do not borrow a penny of this money for anything other than startup costs, no matter how dire your personal financial situation may be.

This half a million is food for the goose that will lay all the golden eggs you need. Don't use $10,000 of it to get your home out of foreclosure, or $2,000 to bail your brother or even yourself out of jail. Breaking your customers' trust and potentially triggering a wave of refunds is much worse than foreclosure or begging family members to scrape together $2,000 to bail you out of jail.

What I'm going to say next may sound paradoxical, but it's necessary. Don't worry about if you can *make money*. Rather, focus on whether your product or service is something people want or need so badly, they will do anything to have it. Even if that means spending their hard-earned cash on it. Focus groups, surveys, and product education are some ways to do this.

So many of us are caught in the catch-22 of "it takes money to make money, but I don't have any money!"

If you noticed, I intentionally avoided talking about saving two years of living expenses, getting loans, and finding wealthy investors.

Why? Well, for one, if you cannot or will not give customers what they want or need, banks or investors could pump $20 million or even a billion dollars into your business, and it will still fail miserably.

The second reason? How many warehouse workers and welfare mothers do you know who can afford to save two years of living expenses or who can qualify for a business loan? How many do you know who will definitely inherit $100,000 in the next ten years?

The answer is somewhere between 1 and -1.

The Best Way to Recover from Recessions

Homeless people and unemployed people can forge alliances with each other to build businesses, especially those in banking, manufacturing, and technology. These industries pump trillions of dollars into the global economy every year for people *to* spend at barbershops, nail salons, and restaurants, as well as on clothing, music, cinema, and sporting events.

Wait, huh? The homeless and the unemployed?

Here's the thing: Even excluding this group's college graduates and former millionaires, the homeless and the unemployed have human capital, the same thing that pulled Japan out of their own "Great Depression," if you will, after World War II. The allies dropped nuclear weapons on Hiroshima and Nagasaki and firebombed everything else in Japan.

They used their human capital to rebuild their businesses, efficiently create quality products, and regain the world's trust. The efficiency piece, in the form of lean manufacturing and 5S, is extensively profiled in the book, <u>The Toyota Way</u>.

In 1959, fourteen years after Japan surrendered and Hitler committed suicide, the United Steelworkers of America went on strike because management teams throughout the industry wanted to implement ways and means to reduce the number of employees needed per unit of production.

The impasse lasted 116 days, or just under four months. However, this was enough time to force automakers and other steel-dependent corporations to import steel from foreign countries, namely Japan and Germany.

In less than fifteen years, men who likely engaged in combat against soldiers from Japan and Germany were inking contracts that enriched steelmakers in these nations.

Furthermore, the quality of steel produced in these nations was superior to that of American steel.

And the rest is history. By the 1980s, Honda took the place of Chevy, while BMW and Mercedes-Benz took Cadillac's place as the ultimate American status symbol. Sony and JVC became as American as Westinghouse and General Electric.

This just goes to show that providing people with high-quality, user-friendly products can turn even the most bitter foes into friends (or frenemies for profit's sake). Talk about strange bedfellows.

So, back to the homeless people and the unemployed people. If they form enterprise-minded collectives with each other, they can employ other homeless and unemployed people and gradually create wealth for themselves as the economy starts to grow.

But they don't have any money!

They can collaborate, grow, and develop today, and worry about funding later, when their efforts have yielded *concrete* plans worth funding.

You must understand, if we wait for rich people and big corporations to expand their businesses and hire more people, any improvements to the economy will only help those who are already rich! These improvements will create more jobs, but not more rich people, if those who already have money are the only ones starting or expanding their businesses.

What about the government? Can't they make jobs? Again, dependence on an entity that already possesses lots of money will not create any new rich people; only those who are already rich will become richer. This means that vulnerable populations are *still just as vulnerable*. Government action to make jobs will just be a pacifier that can be yanked out of the mouths of the vulnerable during the next Congressional budget fight.

Another thing: If you are homeless or unemployed, you have nothing to lose by collaborating with other people in your shoes and working to build something great, anyway. You have more time and mind freedom to devote to a business than someone working a job to keep their home.

Why Do the Poor Get Poorer?

Ironically, it is because those without money focus too much on making money. Wait, how is this even possible?

You see, people who become rich usually work to create a large, lasting impact on their community, society, or the world. For example, in an interview entitled, *James Brown – The Raw & Uncut Interview* (1987), courtesy of *The Best of Vox Pop*, James brown mentioned that he initially made music because his "ambition was to eat; we were very hungry. We were very poor people, and singing was one way I was able to earn a living."

At one time he was very poor and lived in a house with over nineteen people. Rent was only $5 per month, and they had a hard time making it. During that time, James tap danced for soldiers and earned $12, allowing the tenants to pay two months' rent. However, he later used his music as a vehicle to deliver messages of pride and unity with songs such as "Say It Loud – I'm Black and I'm Proud."

He wanted to spread such messages because "if a person is not proud of themselves, if they get frustrated, they can get very, very detrimental to humanity in so many different ways." Furthermore, he believed that if people are proud, their frame of mind is, "I'm worried about what I'm trying to do, trying to make myself better."

Incidentally, his music from the '60s and '70s inspired Prince and Michael Jackson to want to be like him, it revolutionized R&B, and it created the massive rap music industry.

Listen to his songs "Try Me" (1958) and "Papa Don't Take No Mess" (1974), and you will hear the difference. In his early songs, he was following trends, and in his later songs he was setting them.

That's all fine and good, but what about rich people like Kevin O'Leary who say it's all about the money? For starters, such people aim to continue working and improving their craft long after they initially become wealthy.

Dr. Dre is an excellent example of this characteristic, while most of us dream of perhaps working really super hard for ten years, retiring in our thirties or forties, and having "so much money, we never have to work again!" Or being a landlord collecting those proverbial "checks in the mail."

Most people who feel this way end up working some random jobs for many decades and eventually qualifying for Social Security benefits. Hey, they never have to work again! Be careful what you wish for.

The FI/RE movement among young professionals today is the only successful spin-off of this mentality. FI/RE stands for financial independence/retire early. As in work a stressful, six-figure job for ten years; sock away every penny; then move someplace super cheap, such as Arizona, New Mexico, Costa Rica, or Gambia; and live off the dividends your savings earn in the stock market, maybe work odd jobs every now and then.

Well, what about rich people who love the lifestyle with the big house and fancy cars? They aim to be the absolute best in their industry. For them, "good enough" is not good enough. "That'll do" just will not do. Regardless of how hard you work, it is difficult to understand this mentality when you are plugging away at some job you don't care for, and you are not seeking to climb the corporate ladder.

Let us use Charlie Mullins of Pimlico Plumbers as an example. The following is based on his interview on the British television show, "Peter Jones Meets." As a young man, Charlie worked for a wealthy plumber. This man had "a nice house, he had a motorbike, he had a car, he had loads of money." In 1978, Mullins started Pimlico Plumbers. Then, in the early 1990s the economy went into a recession and business fell through the floor, leaving him saddled with debt. He had two options: liquidate everything and close up shop, or double

Why Do the Poor Get Poorer?

down and turn his company around.

He chose the latter.

Charlie replaced all his old staff. In his words, they were "the wrong people." Mullins required his new plumbing staff to be clean shaven, wear clean uniforms, and drive immaculate work vans. ***No exceptions.*** He put his new set of rules in a book called "the Pimlico Bible." Although he liked the big house his former boss owned, he was able to empathize with the customer. He realized that many customers would feel a bit uncomfortable with some scruffy bloke "turning up in a dirty old van, his ass hanging out his trousers."

Good for him. What else causes the poor to get poorer? Believing it takes money to make money and trying to do everything yourself.

Although things cost money, you won't get anywhere if you think it takes money to make money, *when you don't have any money!* Just remember the platitude, "There's more than one way to skin a cat." Paying customers have all the money your business will ever need.

Though trying to do everything yourself can prevent you from being burned by a business partner, it also prevents you from building a great team such as the one that enabled Steve Jobs to turn Apple into a billion-dollar, publicly-traded company at age twenty-five in 1980.

This team was way more people than the two Steves, Jobs and Woz. They risked everything on a new industry that could have easily ended up a dud or a fad, and this brings us to the next point.

Most of us will work hard and, more importantly, be consistent with something if it is guaranteed to make money. Your own startup is not guaranteed to give you any money, and real estate is somewhat guaranteed.

A job with a successful corporation, however, is guaranteed to give you money, despite the talk of job insecurity since the 1980s. That talk just convinces people to pay money to attend wealth-building seminars and get pumped up one weekend. All you have to do is break your back or answer phone calls eight to twelve hours a day, and you get a guaranteed $400 a week.

No wasting time, money, or energy on some business that may (or may not) work out. The Steves and others like them had the guts and the gumption, in the 1970s, to push forward with devoting their lives to the personal-computer industry when its future was as clear as mud. Steve Wozniak, in his early twenties, resigned from his beloved engineering position with Hewlett-Packard paying $25,000 a year, equivalent to six figures in today's money. All for a big maybe. In a November 2006 Talk at Google, he mentioned that Apple's first order of $50,000 was twice his annual salary with Hewlett-Packard.

Poor Bill Gates. Writing code eighteen hours a day, sleeping in some fleabag motel in Albuquerque with Paul Allen when all he had to do was stay at Harvard and get some cushy job at IBM. Bill Gates' mother, Mary, and IBM CEO John Opel both served on the national United Way committee in 1980.

Another thing: The poor focus too much on how they are different from their idea of rich people. As an example, some African Americans talk about "old, rich white guys who inherited money." Meanwhile, low-income Caucasians who did not inherit anything simply talk about "rich people," crony capitalism, or something else the average white person cannot take advantage of.

Stop caring about what you don't have and use what you do have, no matter how little, until you get where you want to go.

If you are serious about developing a new way of thinking conducive to reaching your highest goals, watch *The Men Who Built America* from the History Channel, and force yourself to see yourself in the wealthy robber barons (plus Henry Ford), who are profiled in this multipart eight-hour docuseries. I will admit, when it debuted in 2012, I dismissed the docuseries as just something else glorifying "those old rich white guys."

You already know how greedy and unscrupulous the robber barons were; now is the time to focus on their ***other qualities*** that made them rich in the first place. Greed and loose morals only allowed them to make a little more money on top of what they would have earned, anyway.

Most greedy, unscrupulous people in those days were mere outlaws.

Look beyond the fact they got started when their respective industries were new. Every generation believes that "all the good ideas are taken," even people way back then. If Mark Zuckerberg had that mentality, there would be no Facebook, and Zuckerberg would not be wealthy.

A Checklist for Starting Your Business

The following is a checklist I gave to a young man who wanted to be a flooring contractor. Read it carefully and apply the lessons to your own life and business.

Visit a real estate investors' association (REIA) and become connected with house rehabbers, general contractors, property developers, construction firm personnel, and successful wholesalers who will likely switch over to rehabbing. These people will need new floors, and just a handful of them could keep you and a small team busy with enough work to make you well off. You can find different REIAs on websites such as meetup.com.

If you need a ragtag crew to help with miscellaneous tasks, groups of men usually camp out in front of Home Depot stores each morning, looking for day work. They will readily jump into the back of a slow-moving pickup truck to be whisked away to your jobsite.

Ask yourself these questions:

1. Do I know how to identify asbestos in buildings with portions constructed prior to 1980?
2. Can I work well with other skilled tradesmen in the compressed timeline that most rehabbers have?
3. Am I willing and able to become a licensed, bonded contractor?

4. Do I know the parts of [my city] with the most feverish gentrification efforts?
5. Am I willing to secure government and corporate contracts so as to recession-proof my business?
6. Do I know building codes for flooring?
7. Am I familiar with good dust control techniques?
8. Do I know how to properly measure angles?
9. Can I read a blueprint?
10. Do I know the right questions to ask a client, so that I give them what they want the first time around?
11. Can I properly articulate and demonstrate what I am going to do once I've asked the right questions?
12. Do I know how to properly estimate the cost of a job?
13. Am I aware of any quality surplus flooring sources cheaper than the big box stores?
14. Is there any skill or technique I can improve upon?
15. Can I address any and all customer questions about flooring?
16. Do I know how to engage followers on social media, as opposed to merely advertising and talking *at* them?

Never, ever listen to the siren's call of real estate investing. You will provide service for many successful real estate investors, some of whom love to talk about making $60k on one deal. Focus on being the best flooring contractor there is. Do that, and you, too, will have an easy time earning $60k in a short amount of time.

Unless that investor is already rich, they have to try to secure debt from sources, often hard money lenders, who exert more control over the rehabilitation of a home than a bank would. This is because hard money lenders tend to be former rehabbers who know what works and what does not. Banks, on the other hand, only care about credit history and outstanding loan balances. Let that headache be the rehabber's problem. You show up to install their floors after they have gone through the hassle of securing the funds with which to pay you and other skilled tradesmen.

A Checklist for Starting Your Business

If you do not have piles of cash sitting around, I would suggest having the customer purchase the materials up front, then pay you for labor. You can transport the materials to make it easier for the customer.

If you find, in your experience, that most customers have a problem with this, you can charge upwards of 30% of the total project cost up front so that you can purchase materials with the customer's money! If the upfront percentage you can charge one customer is not enough to purchase all the materials for that person's job, you can talk to multiple clients in the same day and collect multiple upfront fees at the same time.

However, you must stagger the start dates so that client #1 will have paid you enough money by the time you have to start on client #2's project, and so on. Have customers and GCs [general contractors] pay you bit by bit after agreed-upon stages of project completion. You can discount your labor for customers with later start dates, so as to make them more comfortable with waiting days, maybe weeks before their project is started. Get everything in writing before you pick up a hammer, period.

Check out the episode of *Blue Collar Millionaires* that profiles a business called The Flooring King, owned by Antonio Sustiel. After seeing this, you should be able to ignore the siren's call of real estate investing. He earns lots of money from his company's floor installation business alone, which does ten to fifteen homes per day. He also liquidates surplus and closeout flooring from manufacturers.

I would also suggest looking up *The Strangest Secret* (forty minutes), *Let's Talk About Money* (fifteen minutes), and *Twenty Minutes that Can Change Your Life*, all by Earl Nightingale.

Final Words of Wisdom

Working for money makes you broke.

Being an entrepreneur is not for 80% of us, even those of us who don't like working for someone else, and that's okay.

Don't lament, leverage instead.

People these days are too lazy to think. Not true. As an entrepreneur, it is *your* job to think for other adults, and to make your product or service as easy as possible for the average person to use and fully enjoy.

Rich people require it of themselves; those who remain poor think, "at least I tried."

If you are struggling in school, don't immediately pair up with a straight-A student who can make the grade without studying; they are wired differently from you. You will only find yourself asking that student, "How do you know so much?"

He or she will not give you a satisfying answer. Rather, pair up with a B-student who actually has to work for their grades. Why? Your most pressing need is to learn how to learn; this is the "hard work" you need to perform in order to raise your grades. The hard-working B-student will do a better job of helping you than the effortless A-student.

Poor people work to make money. Rich people work to win.

Learn how to be rich from all rich people, even ones you dislike or disagree with.

It takes no courage, effort, or creativity to look for or find "what's wrong" with people, society, so on. It is easier for us to focus on the negative.

Take the time to transform yourself into someone who embraces mistakes as strongly as you embrace glory. It is the only way to avoid going insane.

Want to think more clearly? Go vegan and stop eating gluten (wheat protein). It works for me. Be careful, as many meat substitutes contain vital wheat gluten. What you put in your mouth affects more than just your weight.

People who remain poor will give something a certain amount of ***time*** (six months, two years, et cetera) before giving up. People who become rich require themselves to ***get good at it***, even with the very real risk of never becoming successful at it.

Don't get high to be more creative; just work at your passion when you are sleep deprived. Controlled sleep deprivation, like getting high, is very effective at altering your sense of reality. This altered sense of reality makes you less afraid of getting things wrong, thereby allowing your creativity to flourish unchained.

You can correct mistakes and make refinements and revisions after you have had some sleep.

Your ability to stay awake can be used as a gauge to determine your level of passion for the activity and becoming good at it. Pick one, maybe two nights a week that lie ahead of days in which you do not have much to do, and let your creative juices flow out all night.

The CEO of a company is terrified of cleaning toilets but is willing to lead adults and be the captain of the ship. The janitor is terrified of leading adults and being the captain of the ship but is willing to clean toilets.

You either get to be *right* (about why it is easier for someone else), or you get to be *rich*. You cannot do both.

You get what your heart truly wants or truly believes is possible, regardless of what your mouth says you want.

You should get a good job, take some vacations, and purchase a house and a cheap late-model car so as to get strong desires for material things out of your system *before* you become wealthy and have more at stake.

The more of yourself you spend, the less money you need to spend to become wealthy.

A good MLM company only has revenue streams, profitable or unprofitable, based on products, services, or education sold *by* its independent business owners (IBOs), not *to* its IBOs.

A good MLM also focuses on developing its IBOs into great salespeople and businesspeople, as opposed to recruiting as many IBOs as possible with talk of financial independence or making extra money.

Furthermore, a good MLM will fulfill sales made by its IBOs as opposed to requiring an IBO to purchase product from the MLM before he or she has made any sales. The latter can be likened to Chris Gardner's experience selling bone density scanners.

Does the average person have a $10-million advertising budget? Of course not. That is why you should create a dialog with your potential clients or customers and use their feedback to "make your product or service so good, it will sell itself," so to speak.

The way to reach your goals is to become at least as excited about the *process you need to follow to reach the goal* as you are about the goal itself.

Don't worry about getting it wrong, just get it.

God gives everyone a mission and a handicap, an impediment to accomplishing that mission. Why? He wants us to grow and change. Having a handicap gives us the opportunity to accomplish said growth and change.

Real entrepreneurs want to add value to an organization or for a customer; everyone else just wants to "make money."

The voice of fear and the voice of weakness disguise themselves as the voice of reason.

When it comes to how we feel or what we want, "I don't know," usually means, "I do know, but I'm not at liberty to discuss it." We say, "I don't know," so as to maintain favor with others, avoid arguments and conflict, and to avoid rocking the boat.

The allure of getting something for nothing, ironically, causes many people to *give* something for nothing. Americans alone give about $80 billion a year to the lotteries but only receive about $25 billion in prizes. The periodic jackpot winner only increases this allure.

In pursuing success, you can be ethical, even kind, but don't be reasonable or realistic. Trying to be "reasonable" or "realistic" will limit you to what's already proven, blocking you from what has yet to be discovered.

It is all within reach; the way to get some of it is to reach for one thing at a time. Otherwise, you will expend all your time and energy in a thousand different directions and get nothing or very little.

Most people care more about money than serving the customer, the art of doing business, and their chosen industry. That is why most people have "too much month at the end of the money," *no matter how much they earn* or how hard they work.

The more you learn about human nature, the more you learn about yourself, good, bad, or indifferent. Use it to your advantage.

As long as you try to avoid mistakes and make it appear as if you have it together, you will never get it together.

If you want a mentor, find someone who is kind but will allow you taste failure and defeat every now and then. A "helicopter parent" mentor who steps in at the first signs of trouble will make you too dependent on him or her.

Asking "stupid questions" makes you smarter, especially if you apply the answers to your life.

Want to write a book like this one? In addition to learning from master authors on sites such as masterclass.com, use your word-processing software's "read aloud" feature to help you edit your book. Listening to your writing will help you correct more errors and make your book flow better than just reading your writing with your eyes.

Finally, read these thoughts and essays at least a few times a year. Some of these truths may seem radical if this is your first time being made aware of them as boldly as I have portrayed them. As you work toward your goals, financial and otherwise, the deeper meaning of the foregoing will become clearer, and your heart will become incrementally more open to accepting these truths and applying them to multiple areas of your life.

✳︎✳︎✳︎

www.ingramcontent.com/pod-product-compliance
Lightning Source LLC
Chambersburg PA
CBHW020456220526
45464CB00002B/1010